unleashing
the
Killer
App

digital
strategies
for market
dominance

LARRY DOWNES
CHUNKA MUI

HARVARD BUSINESS SCHOOL PRESS
BOSTON, MASSACHUSETTS

Library of Congress Cataloging-in-Publication Data
Downes, Larry, 1959–
    Unleashing the killer app : digital strategies for market
dominance / Larry Downes and Chunka Mui.
        p.   cm.
    Includes index.
    ISBN 0-87584-801-X (alk. paper)
    1. Information technology—United States—Management. 2. Digital
communications—United States—Management. 3. Organizational
change—United States.   I. Mui, Chunka, 1962–   . II. Title.
    HD30.2.D68   1998   98-11311
    658.4'038—dc21   CIP

*The paper used in this publication meets the requirements of the
American National Standard for Permanence of Paper for Printed
Library Materials Z39.49-1984.*

The movement from unity to multiplicity, between 1200 and 1900, was unbroken in sequence, and rapid in acceleration. Prolonged one generation longer, it would require a new social mind. As though thought were common salt in indefinite solution, it must enter a new phase subject to new laws. Thus far, since five or ten thousand years, the mind had successfully reacted, and nothing yet proved that it would fail to react— but it would need to jump.

—Henry Adams, "A Law of Acceleration" (1904)

contents

foreword

YOU CAN SEE THE FUTURE best through peripheral vision.

Sometimes, looking straight ahead—even with the most dedicated attention and seasoned experience—just misses both the big picture and the new ideas, because they often come at you from those outlying areas affectionately called "left field." Ironically, the more successful that you and your company are, the more likely that you'll miss those seemingly orthogonal ideas. Success can be your worst enemy.

Enter Downes and Mui. They turn your head by asking you to suspend judgment for a little while and to peer with them under the hood of the digital marketplace. If you don't change your gaze willingly, then they'll wrench it away with such one-liners as: "Cannibalize yourself rather than be eaten." You'd better believe it. It is time to understand the digital world even if you are not part of the Nintendo generation.

I comprehend something best when I can explain it in a few simple words. Describing the world in terms of "bits and atoms," as I did in my book *Being Digital*, provided those words. In fact, as a description of the digital world, the "bits and atoms" distinction has improved, not weakened, over time. People quickly grasp the consequences of those 1s and 0s that have no weight, no size, no shape, and no color, and can travel at the speed of light.

Just to name a few: your marginal cost to make more bits is zero. You need no inventory. You can sell them *and* keep them for yourself at the same time. The originals and the copies are indistinguishable. They don't stop at customs. Governments cannot tell where they are. Regulators cannot determine their appropriate jurisdiction. The global marketplace for bits welcomes even the smallest company.

In my lifetime, I've never seen hype and understatement walk hand in hand. But that's what we are seeing now. I'm convinced that our great-grandchildren will look back and wonder why we didn't get it. Why did great-grandma and great-grandpa not see this huge storm coming? On October 15, 1987, I landed in London on a rainy night. The TV weatherman on the 11:00 P.M. news said that tomorrow would be "cloudy with scattered showers." The next morning I awoke to the aftermath of England's biggest hurricane this century, which had uprooted half the trees in Hyde Park, among other things. How did forecasters miss that one?

As this book suggests, classic economic models and traditional business practices are subject to similar upheaval, easily a force 10.0 on the Richter scale of change. One of the reasons why we don't see this tempest clearly yet—why we still think of it as cloudy with scattered showers—is that the digital marketplace is currently small, inconsistent, and in the hands of young people with mostly modest disposable incomes. In fact, if you look at the demographics of the World Wide Web, you'll notice that only a few people between the ages of thirty and sixty use it. The rest of that age group, which I call the "digital homeless," claims to be too busy. The real reason is not a lack of time, nor is it education or income. It is simply that they arrived on this planet too soon to be naturally digital.

Any parent knows all too well how fast children grow up. They are your market force; not just as buyers of tomorrow, but as influencers, trend setters, and teachers of today. My advice to any non-digital CEO (that is, most CEOs) is to ignore their information technology department and "get a kid." Learn about the digital world as a way to connect your family. Then return to your company and challenge your IT department to do something really difficult. If IT says that it is possible, then you have not asked for enough.

You'll realize this in the stories that follow in this provocative book. If the anecdotal evidence does not persuade you, then remember that the fundamental difference between a dog and a human being is simple: When you point with your finger, the dog looks at the tip. The human looks toward the direction in which you point.

Nicholas Negroponte
Cambridge, Massachusetts

preface

OUR WORK OVER the last several years has concentrated on finding ways for companies not just to survive but to exploit dramatic changes in their markets brought on by digital technology. Neither of us began this journey casually. After investing nearly a decade each developing large-scale information systems as consultants with Andersen Consulting, we became frustrated by the failure of such systems to achieve anything more than incremental improvements in our clients' operations. We then began separate quests for a better way. For Larry Downes, this pursuit included stints at the strategy giant McKinsey & Co. and at a Silicon Valley law firm. For Chunka Mui, the process included work with CSC Index during its pioneering efforts in business process reengineering.

We resumed our collaboration at Index Vanguard, which Mui cofounded in the early 1990s. Vanguard was a unique environment, a research forum where representatives from more than a hundred companies from the

United States and Europe came together to explore emerging trends in digital technology. Vanguard's faculty included some of the best-known technologists in the world, such as Nicholas Negroponte, founder of the MIT Media Lab; Alan Kay, the father of the personal computer; Gordon Bell, computer architect and venture capitalist; Robert Lucky, the head of research at Bellcore; David Reed, former chief scientist at Lotus; and John Perry Barlow, former lyricist for the Grateful Dead and a leading voice in the politics of the emerging digital environment he dubbed cyberspace (borrowing the term from William Gibson's science fiction novel *Neuromancer*). A visiting cast of inventors, entrepreneurs, social commentators, and senior executives with stories to tell fed research into topics that included the development of new media, the rise of wireless communications, the role of supercomputing, and the problems of security and privacy in electronic commerce.

During our time together at Vanguard, we came to see how dramatically and rapidly the world was changing and how outdated and even counterproductive many of the basic tools of strategy, planning, and information systems development had become. New electronic markets were appearing overnight, under the radar of anyone's long-range plan. The newest technological innovations began not in the corporate arena, where our clients lived, but in consumer markets, where game computers offered children substantially more processing power (and more compelling applications) than the desktop computers of senior executives. Proprietary computer and communication networks, which we built to link organizations together with their subsidiaries, customers, and suppliers, suddenly looked more like liabilities than assets in the wake of the Internet's explosive growth and incredible interconnectivity.

Technology was no longer the solution. It had become the problem.

As technology became more disruptive, it became clearer that helping our clients understand new technologies was not enough. They needed to see how these dramatic developments would alter not just their plans but the ways in which they develop their plans. Our clients needed to learn how to take advantage of new technologies to create new goods and services and to thrive in, rather than simply endure, the new business environments these developments create.

We left Index Vanguard and developed the basic outlines of digital strategy, an approach to developing and unleashing what we will later describe as "killer apps." We have spent the last two years testing and refining this new discipline; Downes as an independent consultant, speaker, and educator, and Mui as a partner with Diamond Technology Partners, an upstart management consulting firm that has embraced the practice of digital strategy. Mui is also the founder of the Diamond Exchange, a think tank that brings business executives together with experts in both technology and strategy. The Exchange's faculty includes not only technologists like Kay, Bell, Reed, and Barlow, but business leaders like Mel Bergstein, Joe Pine, John Sviokla, Marvin Zonis, and learning guru Tim Gallwey.

In the course of developing our ideas, we have interviewed dozens of senior executives and studied organizations that have won enormous victories or suffered humiliating defeats in their efforts to tame digital technologies. We have worked with leading companies to develop digital strategies and to improve their ability to spot, internalize, shape, and exploit the killer apps that might otherwise have been their undoing.

These clients include manufacturers, distributors, retailers, utilities, banks, government agencies, and publishers—companies whose products include everything from gasoline to Swiss bank accounts to bathroom tiles to french fries. Their digital strategies include building partnerships with their customers, developing information-based products that can be sold and delivered over public data networks, and transforming their businesses from producers of commodity goods to providers of sophisticated services. Along the way, these organizations have changed their structure, their revenue models, and, without fail, their attitude toward the appropriate uses of digital technology. They have remade their own worlds and, we suspect, yours too.

acknowledgments

W E HAVE BEEN blessed with the assistance of many colleagues and friends in the writing of this book. They have given their time generously, for which we can only offer in return our sincere thanks. The development of the ideas, frameworks, and principles in this book have themselves been the beneficiaries of Metcalfe's Law; the more we spread them around, the more value we saw added by the commentary, correction, and augmentation of others.

We first thank those friends who have suffered through nearly every draft of our proposal and manuscript. We owe special thanks to David Reed, who read every draft, as well as Tim Andrews, Gordon Bell, Craig Elderkin, David R. Johnson, Andy Lippman, Joe Pine, Richard A. Posner, and John Sviokla. We received valuable suggestions for improvement from Nicholas Negroponte and Ronald H. Coase, both of whom have demonstrated endless supplies of patience in trying to educate us on technology and on economics, respectively.

In developing the ideas in this book, we have benefited from years of association with Alan Kay, Mel Bergstein, John Perry Barlow, and, more recently, Tim Gallwey and Marvin Zonis. We are also indebted to many at Diamond Technology Partners who provided not only real-world validation of the concepts and principles we describe but often detailed suggestions for improvement during the writing process: Hector Ayala, Julie Brej, James Brock, Paul Carroll, Chris Curran, Steve Farwell, Woody Forsythe, Phil Frank, Pat Gannon, John Erik Garr, Kevin Grieve, Adam Gutstein, Carl Hayes, Jay Kingley, Julian Lloyd, Brad Mart, Jim McGee, Mike Palmer, Tim Rohner, Ken Sansom, Tanya Schuler, Shereen Shermak, Mark Siefertson, Jim Spira, Barry Uphoff, and Tom Weakland.

We would also like to thank our colleagues and friends at CSC Index and, in particular, the staff, advisers, and members of Index Vanguard who helped to shape our early perspectives.

We benefited most from our engagement with key clients, who have worked with us to define a new kind of strategic planning. At VEBA AG our thanks to Ulrich Hartmann, Axel Pfeil, Anton Setter, Ludwig Hoffmann, and, in particular, Jürgen Ziehfreund, who has been an enthusiastic and tireless source of counsel. At McDonald's we thank Carl Dill, whose personal conviction led to the genesis of these ideas and whose careful reading of the manuscript added considerable value. We had generous assistance at British Petroleum from John Browne, John Cross, Martyn MacPherson, Vinod Mehta, Chris Brennan, and, in particular, Phiroz Darukhanavala. At the British Post Office, our thanks to Alan Shepherd and Duncan Hine, as well as all the participants on our 1996 Technology Study Tour.

Thanks are due to other executives who have graciously read and commented on the manuscript itself, including Lauralee Martin of Heller Financial Services, Rakesh Kaul of Hanover Direct, Susan Arseven of Union Camp, Bob Evanson of McGraw-Hill, Vita Cassese and Rich Lynn of Pfizer, and Ken Kruschel of NBC.

Executives at several technology companies have provided us with information and access vital to our case examples. We thank Mike Backes of Rocket Science Games, Bill Gates of

Microsoft, Ed LaHood of Platinum Technologies VREAM labs, and Dick Costolo of Digital Knowledge Assets. We also thank the 423 executives who participated in the Diamond Technology Partners Digital Strategies Survey.

At Harvard Business School Press we owe many thanks, in particular to our editor Kirsten Sandberg and publisher Carol Franco for their support and enthusiasm for the project. Our agent, Raphael Sagalyn, not only ably represented our interests but did extra duty as reviewer and counselor, helping us through several drafts.

For help and hospitality in the process of researching and writing, our thanks to Barbara Ullman, Ed Novak, Kelda Sims, Kevin Morison, Ellen Leander, Alex Moore, Neil Verplank, Scott D. Westrem, Tom Geoghegan, and Lynn Parks-Carter. Particular gratitude is owed to Oliver Blum, our remarkable research assistant, and Richard Bessman, whose editorial suggestions made the book far more readable.

Beth Jenkins offered constant moral support and patience as wife to one of us and friend to the other.

unleashing
the
Killer
App

introduction

THE HISTORY of technology has been a history of dramatic and unexpected consequences. From the Welsh longbow, which decimated the French at Agincourt and effectively ended the Feudal Age, to Edison's lightbulbs, an invention (as recent research in sleeping disorders suggests) that hasn't even appeared yet on the radar of human evolution, change often occurs not slowly and incrementally but discontinuously and in big leaps. The arch, the pulley, the compass, eyeglasses, moveable type, the steam engine, the cotton gin, asphalt, the Model T, elevators, structural steel, the atomic bomb: these are inventions whose impact has extended far beyond the activities for which their creators built them. Ultimately, the havoc they visited on social, political, and economic systems has outweighed the impact of their intended usage.

The investment community that has grown up around technology centers like Silicon Valley and Boston's Route

128 has a name for such inventions. They call them killer applications or, more affectionately, "killer apps." A killer app is a new good or service that establishes an entirely new category and, by being first, dominates it, returning several hundred percent on the initial investment. The personal computer, electronic funds transfer, and the first word processing program are all examples of killer apps.

Killer apps are the Holy Grail of technology investors, the stuff of which their silicon dreams are made. In the coffee shops and juice bars that line Palo Alto's University Avenue, you can always hear someone talking animatedly about the first big spreadsheet or desktop-publishing program, generation-defining video games like Sonic the Hedgehog and Doom, or the first Apple Macintosh, which redefined the very notion of a human-computer interface. Ah, that was a killer app. And now I have one just as good.

For our clients, typically senior executives of large corporations with international operations, killer apps are not seen as such beneficent creatures. Invariably, killer apps wind up displacing unrelated older offerings, destroying and re-creating industries far from their immediate use, and throwing into disarray the complex relationships between business partners, competitors, customers, and regulators of markets. Think of the World Wide Web, for example, and the far-flung predictions for its impact on everything from financial services to manufacturing, from government to the computer industry itself.

Killer apps can create fabulous wealth and breathe new life into a stale economic system. But like the Hindu god Shiva, they are both regenerative and destructive. It is not for nothing that they are called killer apps: our clients are often the companies most likely to be bumped off.

Where do killer apps come from and why do they seem to be arriving in increasing numbers? We describe the process in Part 1, "Digital Strategy." The primary forces at work in spawning today's killer apps are both technological and economic in nature. In bringing the two together in this book, we explain not only what is happening but suggest as well a way to regain your sense of balance, if not control.

The technology we are concerned with is the transformation of information into digital form, where it can be manipulated by computers and transmitted by networks. The driving force behind this transformation is the remarkable science of semiconductors, which has shifted the world's economy from an industrial to an information base in a little over a quarter of a century. The unrelenting, exponential improvements in semiconductor speed, size, and cost that have operated since the 1960s follow Moore's Law, a prediction by Intel founder Gordon Moore that every eighteen months, for the foreseeable future, chip density (and hence computing power) would double while cost remained constant, creating ever more powerful computing devices without raising their price. Announcements from IBM and Intel in late 1997 suggest that Moore's Law may even underpredict the improvement for the next several years. Similar phenomena have been observed by Gordon Bell in data storage and communications bandwidth. The bottom line is simple but potent: *faster, cheaper, smaller.*

Less well known than Moore's Law is the observation made by Robert Metcalfe, founder of 3Com Corporation, that networks (whether of telephones, computers, or people) dramatically increase in value with each additional node or user. Metcalfe's Law values the utility of a network as the square of the number of its users, and can be easily appreciated by considering the impact of standard railroad gauges, Morse code, and standardized electrical outlets in the last century and telephones, fax machines, and the Ethernet and Internet protocols today. Once a standard has achieved critical mass, its value to everyone multiplies exponentially.

Since the early part of this decade, Moore's Law and Metcalfe's Law have operated together in remarkable new ways. Moore's Law made possible the cheap digitization of nearly every device we can think of, from the toaster to the automobile, children's toys, toilets in public buildings, and, of course, ever more powerful and ever more affordable personal computing devices. The proliferation of information devices led to a search for unifying standards that would allow them to share their digital contents and multiply their value in the process. These standards have now arrived, and came not in the form of proprietary architectures from traditional computing and communications powerhouses like IBM and AT&T but from a sleepy U.S. government-built network called the Internet, whose very openness was the single most important factor in its success. In 1993 the Internet's communications protocols reached critical mass, and since then the value of each additional node and user was so great that it began to exert something like a gravitational pull, sucking in every device and network in its path.

With this inexpensive global computing environment in place, Moore's Law and Metcalfe's Law have begun to feed off each other. New software products and standards can be released into the Internet and distributed so cheaply that developers gladly give their products away in order to reach critical mass quickly. This small investment, as Metcalfe predicts, means future users will adopt products with increased enthusiasm (and therefore potential marginal revenue). New computing devices, such as video games, personal digital assistants, and home appliance networks are being built with Internet connections, allowing them to be both users and suppliers of the growing warehouse of global information, much of it freely available.

In addition to improving overall social welfare by creating what economists call "public goods," this inexhaustible and increasingly valuable information base has another, more daunting economic effect. By making it easier for people and the devices they use to find, use, share, and add to the information base of the network, the Internet has developed into a commercial environment, an open market in the truest sense of the word.

This new market, which Harvard Business School Professors Jeffrey Rayport and John Sviokla have dubbed the "marketspace," now challenges the very foundation of modern industrial organization. In 1937, a young economist named Ronald Coase observed that the then recent phenomenon of complex, geographically dispersed firms was a result of market inefficiency. Firms organized, Coase wrote, to reduce the transaction costs of repeated and complicated activities involved in creating, selling, and distributing their goods and services.

The market today is improving its efficiency at the speed of Moore's Law and with the effectiveness of Metcalfe's Law, moving it ahead of Industrial Age firms whose long histories of anti-competitive regulation and whose aging and expensive technology infrastructure keep them from adopting new hardware, software, and standards at anywhere near the pace of the market itself. As the lightning-fast deployment of Netscape's Navigator product for accessing the World Wide Web suggests, the market can achieve critical mass in a matter of months or even weeks. Firms, meanwhile, struggle for months or years just to install the latest release of the Windows operating system or an application suite like SAP.

This increasing adoption gap leads us to what we call the Law of Diminishing Firms, which turns Coase's original observation on its head. As the market becomes more efficient, the size and organizational complexity of the modern industrial firm becomes uneconomic, since firms exist only to the extent that they reduce transaction costs more effectively. Trends toward downsizing, outsourcing, and otherwise distributing activities away from centralized to decentralized management support this view. These trends will only accelerate in the coming years. Firms will not disappear, but they will become smaller, comprised of complicated webs of well-managed relationships with business partners that include customers, suppliers, regulators, and even shareholders, employees, and competitors.

There is more. In addition to wreaking havoc on the organization of firms, the interaction of Moore and Metcalfe is creating powerful second-order effects that unintentionally challenge the basis of business systems in general, as well as social, economic, and even political systems. Consider the steam engine, which opened the American West, but in doing so unsettled the political equilibrium between North and South, forcing the long-deferred resolution of the slavery question. Similarly, today's digital revolution generates considerable stress as it interacts with systems that are slower to change. The Web is currently tearing apart the financial services and telecommunications industries, among others, inspiring civil wars there much as the steam engine did years ago.

The digital revolution's velocity and trajectory create more frequent and more disruptive ripples than did earlier technologies, giving everyone a permanent case of what Alvin Toffler many years ago termed "future shock." We call this phenomenon the Law of Disruption, which states that where social systems improve incrementally, technology improves exponentially. As the gap between the two increases, so does the potential for noncontinuous, disruptive, indeed revolutionary change.

Digitization spurs on already potent trends toward rapid deregulation of industries and globalization of markets, creating a powerful trio of new forces that overpower the traditional competitive threats that a generation of senior executives, managers, and strategists have been trained to follow. To see these disruptive new forces in action, we need look no further than where we started. Killer apps are examples of the Law of Disruption in action, a use of technology whose novelty turns the tables on some previously stable understanding of how things work or work best. In business, killer apps undermine customer relationships, distribution networks, competitor behavior, and economies of size and scale. Killer apps create global competitors where only local players previously mattered. They give customers, suppliers, and new entrants power, upsetting the careful cultivation of competitive advantages that were themselves based on technology, technology that is now suddenly obsolete.

For creative entrepreneurs or executives with an entrepreneurial spirit, the new forces release the potential for radical improvement in their organizations' ability to survive and thrive in the new competitive environment. To do so, however, they must start by jettisoning much of what they know about planning and strategy, adopting a new model we call digital strategy.

In Part 2, "Designing the Killer App," we demonstrate digital strategies in action. From Moore, Metcalfe, Coase, and our own Law of Disruption we distill twelve key design principles for developing, encouraging, or simply taming killer apps. We demonstrate these principles with examples from more than a hundred different organizations in a wide variety of industries.

The design principles are described from the outside in: moving from the organization's environment, through the interface between the organization and its business partners to the core of the organization itself. Following the metaphor of a construction project, we show how the new physics and economics of the digital age require new tools for selecting and assessing sites, for designing new structures that distinguish organizations through their architecture, and for rehabbing the interior spaces of the existing organization to meet the needs of a new generation of inhabitants.

Part 3, "Unleashing the Killer App," describes how digital strategy integrates the new rules with an organization's planning processes. Our focus is on the early stages: the learning, collaborating, prototyping, and strategy design rather than the actual implementation and deployment of killer apps. In our experience working with clients on digital strategy efforts and studying the successes and failures of other organizations, we have learned that these early activities are the hardest and most important.

They are hard not only because they require creative idea generation and testing processes but because they often greatly accelerate an organization's movement from Industrial Age to Information Age. They are important because killer apps are made less often than they are discovered, and the organization with the healthiest environment for identifying, nurturing, and redefining killer apps, whether their own or those invented by others (perhaps for entirely different purposes), is the organization that will translate its digital strategy into market dominance.

To unleash killer apps you must learn to see them coming and be prepared to put together whatever laboratories, partnerships, and new business models are needed to make quick use of them. Before someone else does.

In the end, digital strategy is not really a planning methodology but a new operating model. Unleashing killer apps requires not only the appropriate technology partners, investment models, and prototyping tools we describe, but the corporate will to make the big leaps and to bridge the gap between incrementalism and exponential change. Without that fearlessness, the killer app you unleash may be your own undoing. What is more likely, however, is that you will never achieve escape velocity from your current paradigm to let one loose in the first place.

We describe the process in broad strokes, and save for another day the detailed technical and sociological study of how today's digital strategies, continually improved, evolve into tomorrow's new industry model and next incarnation of your own organization. To give you some sense of the entire life cycle, however, we take you inside a few leading global corporations and show how they abandoned their old, static processes for developing strategy and learned to think creatively, becoming organizations that are nimble, open, even fun. These companies are turning their digital strategy projects into a new incarnation of the organization itself. In so doing, they become companies that live in the future, maximizing their chances for unleashing killer apps.

Our hope is to give you the power to do the same.

digital
strategy

WE LIVE IN an age of anxiety, where rapid changes to social, economic, and political systems—mischief shaped by digital technologies—have left most business people feeling dazed. The chief culprits are disruptive forces we call killer apps—new information technology goods and services that change the rules of the game for people who aren't even remotely connected to the killer apps' intended markets. New killer apps are coming faster all the time.

The goal of developing a digital strategy is to turn anxiety into an advantage, by replacing current planning and strategy activities with new ones better suited to a business environment populated by killer apps. First, though, we need to understand how we got into this mess. Three

11

primary principles—Moore's Law, Metcalfe's Law, and the economic theories of Ronald H. Coase—will get you most of the way there. Moore's Law explains how computers, telecommunication services, and data storage systems defy the laws of gravity and commerce, becoming faster, cheaper, and smaller, all at increasing velocity. Metcalfe's Law demonstrates why these technologies have a tendency to spread quickly and how they move from early adoption to widespread acceptance in great leaps rather than smooth intervals. Coase explains the economics behind this behavior, the clearest explanation we know for the disruptive influence killer apps have on long-standing business traditions and the most stable industries. Putting the three together, the short answer is that for today's killer apps Moore's Law makes it possible, while Metcalfe's Law makes it profitable.

Chapters 1 and 2 present a framework for understanding how these principles apply in today's business environment. Chapter 3 introduces digital strategy, an approach to planning that exploits rather than reacts to the most unstable features of this new world.

1

the killer app

The world now runs on Internet time.
—Andy Grove

Christopher Brennan wasn't trying to start a revolution. The regional manager for British Petroleum's (BP) sixteen hundred gas stations in Germany, Chris was looking for new sources of revenue in a saturated, largely commodity-priced business dominated by a few brands. Then he got an idea. Gas stations were exempt from Germany's rigid shopping laws that required stores of all kinds to close by 6 P.M. during the week and by 2 P.M. on Saturday. Small convenience stores attached to the stations already sold basic staples and impulse food purchases 24 hours a day. Why not really exploit this regulatory loophole? Chris had heard about the future of electronic shopping from his colleague Matthias Richly. Why wait for the future? Why not invent it now?

Working with discretionary marketing funds (and largely on personal time), Chris and a small team created the BP multimedia shopping kiosk, a brilliant combination of digital technology and strategic partnerships with name-brand merchants and credit card companies eager to try a new marketing channel. At the kiosk, consumers use a touch-sensitive screen to view short videos, select merchandise, and get advice on everything from party planning to the latest fashions. All goods ordered at the kiosk could be picked up the next day at the gas station or in some cases even delivered to the customer's home.

Early reception to the kiosk was enthusiastic. German shoppers, assumed to be hostile both to technology and to new services, embraced the kiosk at once. They seemed delighted to be able to order everything for a birthday party or a brunch, based on the recommendations of two-dimensional images. They confounded traditional marketing dogma by using the kiosk to purchase precisely the kind of goods that no one expected anyone would want to buy off a computer screen in a smelly gas station— fruits, vegetables, and even meats. Shoppers began to use the kiosk to replace, rather than supplement, their regular grocery shopping. German consumers, it turned out, were fed up not only with the inconvenient shopping hours but with the quality of their shopping experience. Now they could avoid the crowds, the dirty stores, and the generally unhelpful attitude of the merchants. The kiosk tapped into a channel that conventional wisdom had told Chris didn't exist.

A month into a pilot deployment in Munich, Chris and his team had redesigned the interface several times and increased the number of participating stations. They began making long-term plans to exploit the stations' prime locations as staging and distribution centers, and to deliver the system itself directly to home computers using public networks. Chris and his team were beginning to see that their project had the potential not just to improve gas station revenues but to re-create the very notion of the "station" and the role it played in the consumer's life.

Then they did something really radical. They told the folks at BP headquarters what they'd been up to.

Is There a Strategy in the House?

Chris's story is a story of digital strategy. A manager suspends his disbelief, looks around at the available technologies that might play some role in his planning, forms a variety of alliances and partnerships, and then executes, fine-tuning the experiment not in the laboratory but in the marketplace, with the customer as a true partner. The final result, at least in this case, may be the worst nightmare not just for BP's competitors but for a wide range of other retailers, wholesalers, and distributors. The kiosk may be, in other words, a killer app.

We have purposefully chosen an example from outside the world of high technology companies to demonstrate the broad reach and applicability of digital strategy. What could be less digital than a gas station? What industry less vulnerable than oil and gas exploration, refining, and retailing? Who less likely to remake the face of the value chain than a lone manager, operating in a country that prides itself on conservatism and adherence to long-established rules of commercial engagement?

But hold on a minute. What does the BP kiosk have to do with business strategy? There was no strategy here, just an idea followed by an experiment. Chris did no long-term planning or detailed analysis of the industry. BP, like all large organizations, has a formal strategic planning process and a group of highly trained planners working away in Britannic House, its showcase corporate headquarters, in London. Chris was only vaguely aware of the planning activities of this group. He certainly wasn't acting on the basis of their recommendations.

Perhaps this is your immediate response. A few years ago it would have been ours. Strategy, after all, is the process that Michael Porter and others have taught us about: careful, analytical, and based on a thorough understanding of current market conditions and leverage points. Strategy is what big companies do from the top down. Strategy takes time to develop, time to execute, time to evaluate. What Chris did wasn't strategy, it was just an application, a reordering of relationships. In a word, it was creative.

In the new world, that is strategy.

The Killer App through History

It is too soon to say whether the BP kiosk, or even some future version of it, will prove to be a killer app, which we defined in the Introduction as a new good or service that single-handedly rewrites the rules of an entire industry or a set of industries. Certainly it has the potential. Over the last two years, electronic commerce, of which the BP kiosk is an example, has been touted as the killer app that will redefine the entire manufacturing-distribution-retail-finance business cycle, creating gigantic new markets while it undermines existing ones. Estimates for the speed and scale of electronic commerce range from the conservative (a few billion dollars by the end of the 1990s) to the extreme (the entire cash economy will go digital), but there's no doubt that it is a force with which to be reckoned. The question is when, not whether, and we suspect that you or someone in your organization is already worried.

Electronic commerce as a killer app is more a combination of digital technologies than any one particular new component, product, or service. Its novelty and its explosive potential come from an innovative mix of applications. These include multimedia interfaces (now combining sound, motion, text, and graphics); high-powered, increasingly cheap capacities for computing, data storage, and telecommunications; new forms of payment such as electronic cash; and improvements in security made possible by advanced encryption hardware and software. Electronic commerce is the sum of these parts, built on top of and delivered over the open, global computer network protocols and shared communications services known as the Internet.

Many more killer apps have arrived already, and still more are on the horizon. Consider the potential impact on your business of any of the following: Internet-ready televisions, cars, and other appliances, low-cost digital cameras, desktop publishing software and personal laser printers, intelligent software agents, and telephone services over the Internet. And how about applications now in development at the world's leading technology labs, such as rooms that respond to where you are and what you are doing, wearable computers, electronic ink, and personal area networks?

We don't know how or whether these developments will ultimately change civilization, let alone your business. It is easy, though, to find examples of killer apps from history that demonstrate just how unpredictable and indirect their impact can be. In *Medieval Technology and Social Change*, for example, historian Lynn White, Jr., studied several inventions from the Middle Ages that revolutionized not only the activities they were intended to affect but society as a whole.

Perhaps the most important of these medieval killer apps was the stirrup, which the Franks—Germanic tribes who ruled central Europe after the fall of Rome—adopted from an Asian design. The stirrup made it possible for a mounted fighter to strike with his lance without falling off his horse, greatly increasing the force that could be put behind such a blow. It proved decisive in the Franks' efforts to turn back the marauding Saracens who invaded western Europe in the eighth century, despite the superior numbers of the invaders.

Charles Martel, leader of the Franks, understood from his victory that the stirrup hadn't simply improved the effectiveness of his forces, as a new weapon or fighting formation might have done. Rather, it changed his entire military strategy. Stirrups made possible a mounted cavalry, a new element in the battle equation, and Charles Martel immediately made them a permanent feature.

Neither Charles Martel nor his descendants probably recognized the longer-term impact of their new technology. To support the specialized fighters of a cavalry, Charles Martel created a new class of landed gentry who had sufficient income from the land he gave them to provide men, horses, and expertise. To do this, he seized some of the vast holdings of the Catholic church, permanently altering relations between medieval church and state. He also created a social and political system in which farming peasants were answerable not only to the king but to the landlords, who became known as knights. In the end, the Pope crowned Charles Martel's grandson Charlemagne the first Holy Roman Emperor, an acknowledgment of the new world order.

Thus the lowly stirrup played a singular role in rearranging the political, social, and economic structure of medieval Europe.

The Holy Roman Empire, in some form, lasted until World War I. Feudalism, the social and economic system that emerged to support the mounted troops, at the time represented a sudden and violent break from tradition. It persisted for nearly a thousand years, long after the actual advantage of the stirrup in battle had been supplanted by numerous other developments. As White concludes, "Few inventions have been so simple as the stirrup, but few have had so cataclysmic an influence on history."

As this story demonstrates, killer apps have important first-order effects, but their second-order effects are even more far-reaching—as well as being unintended. In 1976, for example, Gerald Ford offered Americans a toll-free telephone number they could dial to share their ideas for "whipping inflation now." Little did he realize that the newly created "800" area code would soon revolutionize telephone sales and service with twenty-four-hour call centers and television home shopping, and create a major source of new business for resource-poor countries like Ireland. Surely IBM never would have believed that its own marketing of a personal computer, with software and hardware from tiny partners Microsoft and Intel, would devastate their mainframe-centered business model and shatter their computer industry dominance in only a few years.

The Digital Age of Anxiety

To see a more contemporary example of the disruptive power of killer apps, we recently visited the headquarters of the U.S. Postal Service in Washington, D.C. There, executives responsible for technology investment candidly revealed that the postal service has developed a scenario that anticipates a complete shutdown of its operations. Having lost the small package and expedited mail delivery segments, the post office now relies entirely on first-class and bulk mail to support its expensive physical infrastructure, including 200,000 vehicles, 800,000 sorters and deliverers, and 36,000 local post offices. First-class mail is in deep decline, and soon business mail and bulk mail may

fall victim to the same competitor: the humble, almost patheti-
cally primitive technology known as electronic mail.

E-mail, a simple hack invented by scientists whose computers
were connected during the early days of the Internet, has
reached killer app status. Millions of messages are now delivered
automatically and virtually without cost every day. By waiting
too long, the postal service has probably missed the opportunity
to offer electronic postmarks, registration, or other authentica-
tion services—from which it could have derived substantial revenue. Postmaster General Marvin Runyon, arguing to Congress
unsuccessfully in 1996 for a major expansion into electronic
messaging, conceded that "the Postal Service faces growing
competition across all product lines" from what he called the
"electronic bypass." Given that the post office has had an unde-
niable legal monopoly on the delivery of first-class mail for the
whole 200 years of its existence, this is a pretty remarkable confession. But E-mail emerged so quickly that there wasn't a
chance to mount a serious challenge. Now the post office doubts
it can even participate.

E-mail is now being adapted for advertising and information
delivery in what is called "push technology." Why just send a
message when you can send an entire digital product—a multimedia experience? Why call and get an answering machine when
you can type a quick note and be confident that it will be
received and answered within a few hours, often automatically
by increasingly smart systems that can "read" and answer the
mail? Why not send everyone in the company a copy of the
complete text of an interesting article, including active hyper-
links to the references, when doing so takes only a few key-
strokes, no matter if the recipients are down the hall or in Sri
Lanka? E-mail, as a killer app, starts by taking out the post office
but may end by redefining human communications.

It isn't only Postmaster Runyon and his staff who are feeling
threatened by looming killer apps but senior executives in every
industry. As part of a Diamond Technology Partners (DTP)
study led by former *Wall Street Journal* reporter and DTP partner Paul Carroll, we interviewed 30 leading CEOs and surveyed

another 400 senior executives in early 1997. The survey measured management perceptions of the threats and opportunities of digital technology and revealed tremendous anxiety over the new roles for technology signaled by developments like the World Wide Web, intranets (internal networks that use Internet software), and electronic commerce.

Confusion was evident in every business and across all industries: Executives agreed that technology was changing the basic economic equation of their business, but at the same time held firmly to the notion that in their own organization technology was only a tool to implement strategy. Nearly a quarter of those surveyed confessed to feeling that the rules of competition were changing, and changing in ways made possible by technologies that they don't feel they adequately understand. More than 35 percent strongly agreed that digital technology had made markets so transparent that global competitors could now spring up overnight. Few executives felt comfortable saying that they knew how to respond to all these changes, and those few who said they did may have been, as Carroll put it, whistling in the dark.

Moore Is Less, and More

This discomfort with technology is the result of the remarkable increase in the speed with which killer apps have been appearing since 1947. That's the year the transistor was invented, the beginning of the digital age. Since then, digital technology has been turning out one killer app after another, coming faster and faster and often, as in the case of electronic commerce, working in combinations. Computing devices get smaller, cheaper, and more powerful, moving from mainframes, minicomputers and workstations to personal computers, notebooks, and personal digital assistants and continue down to computers in cars, in consumer appliances, in roads, in credit cards, and even in clothing. These devices combine with databases, multimedia interfaces, and communications software to create specialized programs for every profession and activity in business life. Daimler-Benz, for example, has already demonstrated an Internet-ready car and in Germany offers wireless on-board computers that use global positioning satellites to give vocal directions to any destination. The global economy is now increasingly ruled by the technology sector, and every industry has been directly altered by it.

A few basic principles explain how it is that digital technology has become the most disruptive force in modern history. The first, which most people are familiar with, is Moore's Law. First articulated more than thirty years ago by an electrical engineer named Gordon Moore, who founded Intel around the same time, Moore's Law is the counterintuitive, wealth-creating, anti-entropy principle that sits, fat, dumb, and happy, smiling like the Cheshire Cat, at the center of the digital universe.

Moore had witnessed the amazing ability of his colleagues to vastly decrease the size of semiconductors (or chips) with each succeeding generation of product, and he determined that the underlying physics of miniaturization had considerable life left in it. As size decreases, power increases geometrically, both because circuits are closer together and because more of them can be placed on a chip. Moore bet his new company on the belief that new generations of chips, with double the power of the previous generation, could be produced every eighteen months. The cost of producing the new chip, according to Moore, would be the same or less than the cost of producing its predecessor, since improvements in manufacturing technology and increased volumes minimized the cost of new facilities. Older chips, produced on equipment already depreciated, would actually get cheaper.

Hence Moore's Law: *Every eighteen months, processing power doubles while cost holds constant.* (See Figure 1.1) Every eighteen months, you can get twice as much power for the same price, or the same power for half the cost—a remarkably simple, but unimaginably powerful equation. Imagine Henry Ford predicting that the internal combustion engine would double its power every year and a half without becoming any more expensive. By now we'd be driving cars that could take us to the moon for lunch. The engines in these vehicles would be given away with the purchase of a Big Mac.

Moore's Law has operated with remarkable accuracy for thirty years and, according to computer architect Gordon Bell, it stands ready to do so for at least another five or six generations of processors. Even in today's most expensive PC, a Pentium processor accounts for less than $100 of the retail price. Moore's Law (for slightly different reasons) also applies to other aspects of digital technology, including computer memory and data storage devices. Telecommunications bandwidth, the speed at which data can be moved through the phone network, is experiencing similar improvements thanks to high-speed fiber-optic cable, satellites, and wireless communications technologies, all of which can be used on the same network.

FIGURE 1.1

Moore's Law

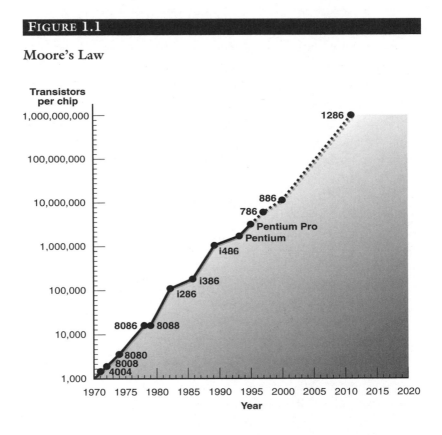

Source: Adapted from Otis Port, Andy Reinhardt, Gary McWilliams, and Steven V. Brull, "The Silicon Age? It's Just Dawning," *Business Week,* 9 December 1996.

Everything having to do with digital technology gets relentlessly faster, smaller, and cheaper. The computer in your cellular phone has more power than all the computers used during World War II combined. In 1980, a gigabyte of storage cost several hundred thousand dollars and took up the better part of a room. It now fits on a credit-card sized device that costs less than $200. Telecommunications technology, with the help of deregulation, has already collapsed the price of long distance calls in the United States. Software applications that had previously proven uneconomical—multimedia interfaces, expert systems, groupware—suddenly have the wherewithal to enter the market, taking advantage of low-cost computing power, memory, and storage to perform complex tasks.

In consumer markets the price decrease is tangible. Personal computers debuted at about $3,000 in 1985; they are now available for less than $1,000 and are, at the same time, several orders of magnitude more powerful. There are now 200 million computers in the world. Go even smaller, and you'll discover that there are probably more than 100 microprocessors in your home. As Moore's Law advances, it costs almost nothing to stick a simple computer in your coffee maker to let you program the time and strength of your morning brew. There are 6 billion such chips embedded inside other devices.

In the future, all the devices you use from day to day will have chips. The chips will be linked, perhaps over the very wires that bring in power, and will communicate both inside and outside your home. The power company will monitor usage and performance on a second-by-second basis, allowing it to balance loads, buy and sell excess power, and provide you and other businesses with valuable data. What starts out as a clever feature of your coffee maker just might create an entirely new industry model for public utilities.

Metcalfe's Useful Equation

Moore's Law goes a long way toward explaining why the digital age is increasingly populated by killer apps. What it doesn't tell you is why these applications seem to spread as quickly as they do. To understand that, you need Metcalfe's Law. Consider the telephone. How useful is it? Your answer depends entirely on how many other telephones there are and on how easily they can be interconnected. One phone is useless, a few phones have limited value. A million phones create a vast network, and a network is something, as the Communist governments of the former Soviet Union learned to their dismay, with tremendous power.

Robert Metcalfe, founder of 3Com Corporation and the designer of the robust Ethernet protocol for computer networks, observed that new technologies are valuable only if many people use them. Specifically, the usefulness, or utility, of a network equals the square of the number of users, a function known as Metcalfe's Law. (See Figure 1.2) The more people who use your software, your network, your standard, your game, or your book, the more valuable it becomes, and the more new users it will attract, increasing both its utility and the speed of its adoption by still more users. If you and I can call only each other, to return to the telephone example, a phone is of little value. But if we can call nearly everyone else in the world, it becomes irresistible.

The diagram of Metcalfe's Law in Figure 1.2 shows a magical point of inflection, the knee of the curve, at which a technology reaches critical mass. After that point, its value increases exponentially. How quickly a new application hits the knee depends on how much it costs new users to get access to the network (for instance, a telephone and monthly connection charges), since buyers will weigh this cost against the usefulness of the technology at the time of purchase. The lower the initial price, the more quickly critical mass is reached. And ironically, once critical mass is reached, the developer can in theory charge subsequent users more, because the network effect increases the application's value.

For the phone system, or the power system, the initial investment in network infrastructure was high, which kept the price of access high. In the case of railroads and telephones, initial developers failed to appreciate the value of interconnection (in essence, the power of the Metcalfe curve). Railroads struggled with multiple gauges of track, which limited connections between systems, until the late 1880s. It didn't even occur to telephone companies to put a dial on the phone until 1931, even though the high cost of employing people as switchboard operators limited the reach of the network. In the predigital age, Metcalfe's Law could take decades to unleash network power.

Developers of today's digital technology are conscious of Metcalfe's Law, and they are developing counterintuitive rules necessary to optimize and exploit it. The most dramatic demonstration of Metcalfe's Law during the digital age has been the explosion in the early 1990s of the Internet, a network of computers and a set of standards that makes it easy for computers to share data. The Internet had existed in various forms for many

FIGURE 1.2

Metcalfe's Law

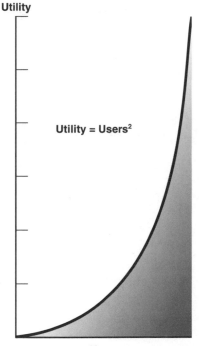

Utility

Utility = Users^2

Users

years, but reached critical mass in 1993. (See Figure 1.3) From there, true to form, the Internet became the "it" technology, attracting not only users but billions of investment dollars, regular cover stories in popular magazines, and even Hollywood movie makers.

FIGURE 1.3

Birth of a Network

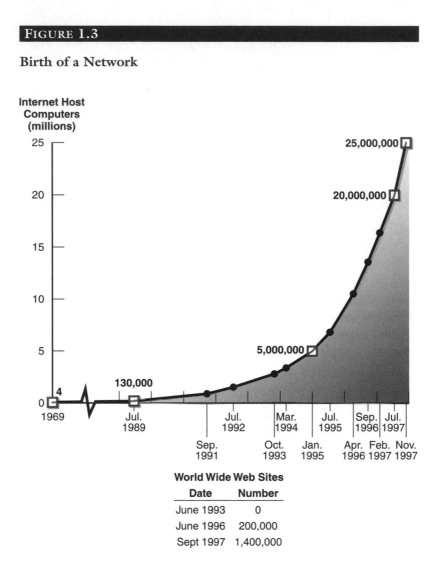

Internet Host Computers (millions)

World Wide Web Sites	
Date	Number
June 1993	0
June 1996	200,000
Sept 1997	1,400,000

Source: The Internet Society, http://www.isoc.org/.

Computer hardware, software, and networking companies had been building up their user bases for decades with closed, proprietary networking standards like IBM's Systems Network Architecture and its PC token ring network, document interchange, and hundreds of subsidiary "IBM solutions"—solutions, that is, for IBM. The Internet, on the other hand, has always been based on open, public standards, allowing it to grow faster despite its lack of a marketing function or, indeed, *any organization whatsoever.* The Internet became the dominant global computing network it now is by being the first to reach the knee in Metcalfe's curve, and the impact of that victory will be played out in the information technology industry for years to come.

The notion that an open system—a system that gladly gives all its secrets away—could humble a giant like IBM seems the stuff of fairy tales. Meet Marc Andreessen, who was an undergraduate at the University of Illinois in the early 1990s when the World Wide Web, a new set of open standards for sending and receiving multimedia communications over the Internet, was in its infancy. In an effort to exploit these standards Andreessen wrote Mosaic, a program that allows users to browse through the various Web sites that were being created. To get maximum exposure for Mosaic, Andreessen lowered the access cost—that is, the price of the software—*to zero.* Even when former Silicon Graphics founder James Clark stole Andreessen and his team away to start Netscape Corporation, the operating model didn't change. Netscape Navigator, the company's rapidly evolving browser, is still being given away.

The result? Netscape captured 80 percent of the browser market within months of its first product release in 1995 by giving away millions of copies of its software. Unlike telephones, giving away Navigator costs little in real dollars. Thanks to the Internet itself, users simply download the software, using their own phone connection, their own machines, and their own electricity. The marginal cost of each "copy" of Navigator that Netscape has given away is not *effectively* zero, it is *actually* zero.

Eighty percent of a market for a free product doesn't sound like much of an achievement, but when Netscape stock debuted in 1995, it went from an initial asking price of $14 a share to $150 in a matter of days, giving the company a market valuation of more than $3 billion dollars. The rapid proliferation of Navigator encouraged faster development of Web sites, which in turn led to greater demand for Navigator. The company now derives revenues from subsidiary goods and services, such as advertisements on its own Web site and information broadcasting services, software tools for building corporate "intranets" (an *intranet* is a network similar to the Internet that operates only within a single organization's defined boundaries), and products that allow developers to build and manage the Web sites that Netscape's "free" users are visiting. Software giant Microsoft arrived late to the market for browser software and the related services it makes possible, but used its own market power (illegally, according to the U.S. Justice Department) to cut into Netscape's dominance in 1997. Still, Netscape reported more than $500 million in revenue for that year.

Navigator hit the Metcalfe curve at warp speed, with critical mass and the predictable explosion occurring not in years but in months. In 1994, when we first demonstrated Mosaic to clients, the World Wide Web was an experiment. By 1997, nearly every network television advertisement included a Web address. What's more, entire industries had sprung up and matured by devoting themselves to creating supplemental software, including audio, video, and three-dimensional modeling tools, as well as services for developing, hosting, and managing Web sites for corporations. The Internet itself is their low-cost channel for advertising, product development, manufacturing, and distribution.

The Law of Disruption, or Second-Order Effects

This is not the world of the future but the one we already live in. As Moore's Law continues its relentless journey into the realm of the smaller, cheaper, and faster, the acceleration of new technology introductions will increase. As it does, Metcalfe's Law is there to spread them around. As Nicholas Negroponte wrote famously in 1995 in his book *Being Digital,* these two powerful principles are driving the transformation of the world from one made up of atoms to one made up of bits. Games, as well as most other forms of entertainment, much of the world's money supply, nearly everything published, corporate knowledge, and most forms of communication are all becoming digital—just to name a few. The digital revolution is scooping up all the information-intensive processes you can think of, and several you can't. This migration of activities, functions, and people from the world of the physical to the world of the digital has created a new environment, which its inhabitants know as cyberspace. "Computing," as Negroponte says in *Being Digital,* "is not about computers anymore. It is about living."

"Atoms to bits" is the second-order effect of the killer apps in the digital age, their sudden and dramatic disruption of the political, social, and economic system. It's already begun, and it will make feudalism look mild by comparison. We refer to these second-order effects, the combination of Moore's Law and Metcalfe's Law, as the Law of Disruption. (See Figure 1.4) It can be simply stated as follows: *Social, political, and economic systems change incrementally, but technology changes exponentially.*

The systems that make up human civilization, including commercial systems, change over time, but they do so on an incremental basis. Law, for example, evolves to encompass the unique features of new technologies, but it does so at an agonizingly slow pace, as anyone who has studied railroad, banking, or telecommunications law can attest. Technology change instead follows the track of Metcalfe's curve. Once there is a critical mass of users, the rate of change—what you might think of as the disruption index—accelerates exponentially. It is in the growing chasm between the different rates of change that secondary effects occur.

Technology change initially affects technology, in other words, but once critical mass is reached, the disruption takes place in other, unrelated systems. Television redefines the relationships of family and community; cloning challenges basic understandings and definitions of character and personhood. Electronic commerce has caught national and local governments completely off guard, and while they scamper to figure out how to apply whomever's law, the technology continues to evolve into forms less and less analogous to enterprises with which they are familiar. These are the types of changes that historian Thomas Kuhn, in a much more limited context, first referred to in 1962 as paradigm shifts, discoveries so fundamental that they knock out the basic pillars of universally held beliefs, requiring that brand new structures be built to explain them. In the case of digital technology, the new structure is called cyberspace.

Cyberspace is not a solid structure located in a certain place, but a collection of digital technologies that together create an increasingly believable illusion of place. The more activities the environment can support, the faster organizations and individuals alike must adapt to its atmosphere, its gravity, and its physics.

FIGURE 1.4

The Law of Disruption

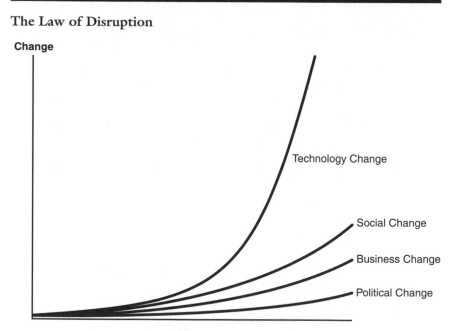

Since corporations are themselves imaginary creatures, doing business in a virtual location requires relatively little in the way of adaptation. But for human beings cyberspace is disorienting. It will take some time to get used to it. The vertigo that nearly everyone—politicians, CEOs, homemakers, and grandparents—first experiences there is the Law of Disruption in action. It is as if one were physically making the leap to the top of Metcalfe's curve.

The Internet as Primordial Soup

Many of our examples of killer apps and digital strategies will come from or be intimately connected with the Internet. This is because the Internet is the closest environment we have today to the world of bits, and it is the place where the missing components, the new technologies, and the new business models are being introduced, tested, and observed. If cyberspace is the world of tomorrow, think of the Internet as a primitive rendering of that world, the primordial soup from which it is emerging.

The Internet began as a collection of research and defense-related networks created under the auspices of the Department of Defense (the U.S. government no longer operates the Internet or provides significant funding for it). The goal of the Department of Defense was to create a computer network that would be indestructible, even in the event of nuclear war, supporting continued command and control activity by the government and the military. Hardly the beginnings of a commercial technology that now threatens to take over the world as we know it.

The key to the Internet's growth, however, has been precisely that design principle of uninterruptibility. To make a network that could not be broken, the designers avoided making any one connection vital. Messages, data files, pictures of your grandchildren—anything being sent over the Net is broken into small packets and routed dynamically from one computer to another, stopping along the way at a number of intermediate relay computers. New York City is wiped out? No problem, the

packets just detour around it. An individual link is down? That's
OK, too, since there are many redundant channels. The Internet
is completely decentralized, and there is no hierarchy among the
various connected computers that make up the network. But
lack of hierarchy does not mean anarchy: fish swim together, after
all, without a chain of command.

The Internet's openness allows it to take optimal advantage
of Moore's Law and Metcalfe's Law. It's open to everything,
and inside its networks there is a fiercely competitive marketplace of ideas, where new standards, products, and information
can be whipped around the world and back in a greatly con-
densed time frame. It is a network that is constantly being
rebuilt, taking advantage of every new advance in digital technology, from high-bandwidth communications (the network
itself is a wild combination of fiber, cable, wire, wireless, satellite,
cellular, and several other communications media), multimedia
user interfaces, global computing architectures, and increasingly
powerful software for sharing information. Product developers
now refer to "Internet Years," roughly equivalent to dog years.
A company that is one Internet year old acts like one that has
been around for seven years.

The Internet, as we will refer to it in the rest of this book, is
the best conduit through which Moore's Law and Metcalfe's
Law are operating together. In this sense it has become, and will
remain, the most potent test laboratory available for new digital
technologies. As we'll discuss in Part 2, the Internet is also the
most important crucible in which to test new strategies and
operating principles that has come along since the open market.

Killer Apps, Take Two

We began this chapter by demonstrating the disruptive power of
killer apps—innovative uses of technology, like BP's kiosk and
Charles Martel's stirrup—that suddenly destroy the equilibrium
of what appeared to be stable systems of commerce and society.
To explain the sudden and alarming appearance of killer apps in
the digital age, we introduced Moore's Law and Metcalfe's Law,

which together account for much of the confusion, a confusion we described as the Law of Disruption.

We have now come full circle. Killer apps are manifestations of the Law of Disruption, the visible catastrophes that punctuate the invisible workings of Moore's Law and Metcalfe's Law, much as earthquakes and volcanoes are the manifestations of complex interactions between geological forces beneath the surface of the Earth. As the rate of technological change increases relative to social rates of change, the incidence of killer apps increases.

Killer apps are the collisions between exponential technology adoption and systems that prefer to change in even, incremental measures. How disruptive they are depends on where in the technology curve they are introduced. E-mail will probably take less time to kill the post office than automobiles took to kill the horse and buggy. As Moore's Law and Metcalfe's Law increase the speed with which the digital killer apps are released, the mean time to death decreases.

But what do killer apps have to do with your business strategy, or, more particularly, with the development of what we referred to as *digital strategy?* Why does it seem that in the last few years digital technologies have been focusing their disruptive power on your industry, your markets, and your organizational structure? To answer these questions, we have to travel back in time again. Not to the Middle Ages, but to 1937.

2

the new economics

I don't know who discovered water, but it probably wasn't a fish.
—Marshall McLuhan

WHAT IS IT ABOUT THE digital killer apps that makes them so deadly? If Moore's and Metcalfe's Laws are improving the power and speed with which technology enters the marketplace, shouldn't that be cause for celebration and not anxiety? Why does the Law of Disruption apply to commerce at all, when conventional wisdom holds that technological innovations improve productivity and create new wealth?

Moore and Metcalfe explain how digital technology spawns so many killer apps, but we need to look elsewhere to understand why business executives now see technology as their main competitor instead of their chief weapon. The answer comes from the remarkable work of economist Ronald Coase. Coase's breakthrough work on transaction costs, as well as the peculiar economics of information provide a powerful framework for thinking about the new economics of cyberspace.

Ronald Coase's Journey

Ronald Coase was in his twenties when he made the most important discovery of his life. He had finished his course work in industrial management at the London School of Economics and decided to spend his last year doing field research. Coase, who was ideologically a socialist, wanted to show that the state could be a more efficient manager of the economy than the free market. To prove it, he came to the United States to study the closest thing he could find to a nonmarket economy—the growing American phenomenon of the firm, exemplified by companies like Standard Oil, General Motors, and U.S. Steel. Inside these increasingly large organizations, the full range of market functions—purchasing, marketing, sales, manufacturing, distribution—were performed internally. Traveling around the country in 1931, at the height of the Great Depression, Coase was struck by the failure of economists to answer a few basic questions: Why did firms form at all? Why were they the size they were and not larger or smaller? How did entrepreneurs decide which functions to bring inside and which to leave to the open market?

It was an eventful trip, and by its end Coase had begun to question his faith in socialism and government regulation. In the process, he made a discovery about market behavior that he published in a 1937 article entitled "The Nature of the Firm." Coase's discovery was of such importance that it was one of only two achievements singled out by the Nobel Committee that awarded Coase their prize for economics over fifty years later. Ronald Coase had discovered *transaction costs*. As we'll see, it is this discovery sixty years ago that explains the new economics of cyberspace. First, though, you need to understand how it is that Coasean economics operates in traditional industrial markets.

Transaction Costs, or The Unnatural Nature of the Firm

To understand the concept of transaction costs, let's take a simple example. Let's say you work for an average-sized firm and you've run out of paper clips. Almost assuredly, you will get your paper clips not by going out on the open market but by going down the hall to the supplies department of your office, which has purchased and maintains an inventory of paper clips in your building. Your company will, in fact, keep such basic supplies on hand as a matter of course, without giving much thought to the cost of carrying such inventory, even if buying and distributing office supplies is not the core activity of your business. Your company is likely to keep paper clips on hand even if there was no discount for buying in bulk.

The reason? Even if you could get paper clips on your own for the same price, you still have to *get them*. This means finding out where the stores that carry them are located and how much they charge, deciding between the closest store and the one with the best price, making sure that you are really charged what the store advertises, and, if the clips are somehow defective, taking them back and demanding replacements or some other remedy.

And that's just for a simple transaction. Imagine instead that you were buying raw materials needed to manufacture your product. There is the additional effort of negotiating a price, writing a contract, inspecting the goods, and, potentially, invoking the legal system to enforce the contract. Better, you say, to own the supplier or at least to buy in bulk and avoid all that trouble.

That "trouble" is transaction costs, a set of inefficiencies in the market that add—or, as Coase argued, should be added—to the price of a good or service in order to measure the performance of the market relative to the nonmarket behavior in firms (or in weighing the costs and benefits of government regulation). There are six basic types of transaction costs:

- **Search costs:** buyers and sellers finding each other inside the increasingly broad and disorganized open market.

- **Information costs:** for buyers, learning about the products and services of sellers and the basis for their cost, profit margins, and quality; for sellers, learning about the legitimacy, financial condition, and need (which may lead to a higher or lower price) of the buyer.

- **Bargaining costs:** buyers and sellers setting the terms of a sale or contract for services, which might include meetings, phone calls, letters, faxes, E-mails, exchanges of technical data, brochures, entertainment, and the legal costs of contract negotiations.

- **Decision costs:** for buyers, evaluating the terms of the seller compared with other potential sellers, and internal processes, such as purchasing approval, designed to ensure that purchases meet the policies of the organization; for sellers, evaluating whether to sell to one buyer instead of another buyer or not at all.

- **Policing costs:** buyers and sellers taking steps to ensure that the goods or services and the terms under which the sale was made, which may have been ambiguous or even unstated, are in fact translated into the real goods and services exchanged. This might include inspecting the goods and any negotiations having to do with late or inadequate delivery or payment.

- **Enforcement costs:** buyers and sellers ensuring that unsatisfied terms are remedied. This could range from mutual agreement on a discount or other penalties to the often high cost of litigation, that is, using an external tribunal to settle disputes associated with the transaction.

As this list suggests, transaction costs range from the trivial (turning over the box to see what the price is) to amounts greatly in excess of the transaction itself (imagine if you were seriously injured by a defective paper clip). In any case, transaction costs add a layer of complexity to market transactions, and Coase thought they would be studied carefully. Yet we know little more today about their nature, size, and avoidability than we did when Coase published his findings in 1937. His fellow economists simply assume their way around him and now study markets and prices under the fiction of a "frictionless" economy (an economy, that is, in which transaction costs don't exist).

Firms are created, Coase concluded, because the additional cost of organizing and maintaining them is cheaper than the transaction costs involved when individuals conduct business with each other using the market. What functions should a firm perform internally? The answer is only those activities that can not be performed more cheaply in the market or by another firm. In fact, as Coase says, a firm will tend to expand precisely to the point where "the costs of organizing an extra transaction within the firm becomes equal to the costs of carrying out the same transaction by means of an exchange on the open market." For some activities, say plumbing, the open market works relatively well, and the need for plumbers to form large firms to avoid transaction costs has never arisen. For the large-scale operations of General Motors and U.S. Steel, which require coordination, heavy capital investment, and complex distribution systems, the firm is the only economically viable solution.

Viable, but not perfect. As anyone who has ever worked for an organization knows, the cost of performing a function inside a firm is the creation of communications and coordination functions, activities known collectively as bureaucracy. Bureaucracy increases as the size and complexity of the firm increases, sometimes approaching or surpassing the alternative transaction costs of the market. We have seen employees using their own travel agents rather than hassling with corporate travel departments, or computing at home where they can avoid the needless oversight of the corporate I/S group. In regulated industries or cartels, where there is no market alternative, customers may simply forgo the transaction—adding a second phone line or changing an airline reservation—rather than fight the inside costs.

Blown to Bits

Even before the digital revolution, technology played a central role in the development of firms. Coase noted in 1937 the enabling role of communications technologies like the telegraph and telephone, which reduced the cost of maintaining a large-scale organization across wide distances and thus made possible the creation of larger firms. Up until now, the role played by digital technology has been consistent with that history. Computers, networks, and large-scale data storage capabilities have made it possible for bigger and more complicated firms to emerge, internalizing more and more market functions and casting their shadow over a wider range of activities in an increasingly global market. According to the Bureau of Economic Analysis, U.S. companies spent $212 billion on information technology in 1996 alone, or roughly 5 percent of the GDP. Think of the global financial markets and their dependence on such technology. They couldn't exist without technology, and they didn't.

Large-scale industrial companies are also in some sense creations of digital technology. One example is British Petroleum, a major oil producer, which coordinates exploration, refining, and retail distribution on a worldwide basis, with major operations in such out-of-the-way spots as Alaska and Vietnam. BP relies on digital technology for everything from selling its products in the commodities markets, to storing and processing enormous quantities of geological data, to hosting regular videoconferences for its experts, senior executives, and exploration teams around the world. New applications, following Moore and Metcalfe, quickly become normal features of daily life. Only a few months after BP launched an experiment in virtual team-working with videoconferencing and other software that enabled teams to share and simultaneously edit documents, diagrams, and other work products, the combined technology became an accepted part of how BP operates.

So it is ironic that the long-standing servant of such firms has now become their worst nightmare. Just as technology reduces the costs of operating a firm, it reduces the costs of the market itself. It's not only firms that get more efficient, in other words; the market is also getting more efficient. Moore's Law and Metcalfe's Law are working to create a new marketplace where transaction costs are reduced not incrementally (as they are in today's firms with reengineering and similar cost-cutting activities) but exponentially. As Harvard Business School professors Jeffrey Rayport and John Sviokla point out, in this evolving "marketspace," it is not only the infrastructure that is different, but the content and context of transactions as well.

Think of the Internet not as a network of connected computers but as the testbed for a new market economy, one that is global, continuously operating, and increasingly automating the processes of buying, selling, producing, and distributing. To return to the paper clip example, instead of leaving the building, you can now simply point yourself to Office Depot's Web site, click on the product you want, give them your credit card number, and get the paper clips the next day via UPS. Soon, that process will be enhanced by intelligent software "agents," such as those being developed by start-up software companies like Firefly, which use sophisticated pattern-matching algorithms to make recommendations based on your past behavior and the behavior of their growing databases of other shoppers.

Buying paper clips on the World Wide Web today is hardly a frictionless transaction, but it's an awful lot closer to it than shopping in the real world. Maybe it's already cheaper than engaging your office bureaucracy.

In the move to the marketspace, dramatic results are already visible. Whole industries, particularly those—like banking, insurance, publishing, and entertainment—that are the most information-intensive are simply being blown to bits. The Law of Disruption is relentlessly opening closed markets, exposing corporate waste, and laughing in the face of government intervention. In the insurance industry, startups like Quickquote are already offering agentless sales for such basic products as term life. Large insurers, at the same time, are constrained by the leverage of more than 650,000 insurance agents in the United States alone. As the CEO of one midsize insurer told us recently, "The industry is so dominated today by distribution that every time management tries to change something, the system of independent agents promptly kicks management in the groin. We feel under siege, and yet we think there's real opportunity here. It's a great time to be a schizophrenic."

The economic disruption caused by today's digital killer apps is twofold, the first a function of Moore's Law and Metcalfe's Law and the second a function of the Law of Disruption:

1. Killer apps are reducing transaction costs, in many cases dramatically, for nearly all goods and services.

2. They are doing so much faster in the open market than they are for firms.

That the market itself could become more efficient by reducing transaction costs is not something Coase has considered, but the result, when the market does, is entirely predictable given the "nature" of firms. If firms increase in size until they reach the point where the next transaction would be just as cheap if done outside the firm, what happens when the outside world gets cheaper? The natural corollary is that the firm shrinks. If Coase is right about the relationship between firms and transaction costs, there is this even more shocking implication, which we call the Law of Diminishing Firms: *As transaction costs in the open market approach zero, so does the size of the firm.*

A truly frictionless economy needs no permanent firms. We don't mean to suggest that such a future is imminent or even possible. For most complex transactions, even the most perfect information flow would still leave considerable transaction costs. The nature of the firm will change, however, and indeed, it is already changing. The concept of a firm as a physical entity, defined by its permanent employees and fixed assets, is giving way to what some have called a "virtual organization," where employees may be part-time or contract workers, where assets may be jointly owned by many organizations, and where the separation between what is inside and what is outside the firm becomes increasingly hazy. Venture capital firms, like Silicon Valley's Kleiner Perkins Caufield & Byers, link the companies they fund into a network, borrowing the Japanese concept of *keiretsu*. Individuals will be participants in many enterprises, like today's entrepreneurs, and those enterprises will be formed around events much closer to transactions than to a sense of corporate immortality.

The Law in Operation Today

Economists have done little to quantify the impact of transaction costs in traditional markets, but you don't have to look far to see the Law of Diminishing Firms turning the marketplace into the marketspace. Information and service businesses, such as dealers, agents, and brokers, are the first victims of reduced transaction costs, since they face head-on the improvements in information exchange. The start-up company Auto-by-Tel, for example, uses the Web to remove many of the expensive and unpleasant transaction costs of buying a car. Visitors to its site review extensive databases to make a selection and are then routed directly to qualified dealers who provide a binding quote within 24 hours. Auto-by-Tel can also provide loans and insurance. The activities of today's car dealer are greatly reduced, and in the end may be eliminated.

There's another group of early victims. Mature industries, regulated industries, and monopolies and cartels, which by definition avoid competition from the open market, have done little to reduce their basic costs. Consequently, they are proving to be not only vulnerable but downright fragile when even a little ray of competition or deregulation sheds light on their operating models. Investment in digital technology is a key feature of competitiveness. These organizations, which include most of the utilities and transportation sectors as well as a large chunk of the retail supply chain, have grossly underinvested and misinvested in technology, making them extremely tempting targets. In Japan, the "Big Bang" deregulation of financial markets that will take place over the next few years has led to a mad rush to upgrade uncompetitive technology infrastructures, with banks, insurers, and securities firms spending more than $11 billion in 1997 alone.

In the United States and Europe telecommunications deregulation is bringing in surprising new competitors for the traditional telcos—cable companies, foreign companies, as well as start-up companies without fixed assets. In Europe, alliances of electric utilities and companies that own large private networks (like the Union Bank of Switzerland, the Swiss railway, and

Migros, the country's largest retail chain, which pooled their assets to form Newtelco) are forming to take on the national carriers. At the same time, technology and content-rich companies like Microsoft and Disney are buying up the technology poor, like Comcast, TCI, and Capital Cities/ABC.

Sudden mergers in formerly stable industries are just one of the most visible trends in today's business environment that can be explained by the Law of Diminishing Firms. Add to that list the disintermediation of wholesalers, the craze for outsourcing, and even much of the downsizing seen in the last ten years. Each of these is, at its core, a response to decreasing transaction costs in the open market.

Mergers and Acquisitions

As transaction costs fall, one of the remaining advantages a firm has over market transactions is the advantage of scale—the ability to outperform the market by saving money through repetition. Most of the interesting recent merger activity has been in industries experiencing sudden changes because of significant deregulation or changing market conditions, as in the defense industry. (As one Brigadier General of the British Army described the end of the Cold War to us: "Our market changed.") It is no coincidence that frenzied consolidation is taking place in banking, telecommunications, and insurance, all of which are responding to the new pressures of a competitive market that has absorbed new technologies more quickly than they did during their regulated slumber.

When banks had a monopoly on certain financial activities, there wasn't much pressure to perform, and branches proliferated. Now that anybody can be a bank for most purposes and can do so cheaply by using ATMs and the Internet, those branches are a significant drain (see Figure 2.1). A merged bank can close redundant branches, which is exactly what Wells Fargo did as part of its hostile takeover of First Interstate in 1995. And Wells Fargo, as we'll see, is also leading the banking industry in new technology investments that may ultimately redefine the concept of banking.

Disintermediation and Disaggregation

A second effect of reduced transaction costs in the market is that they force the participants in stable industries to reconsider who is capturing the margins. Nearly every distribution activity, from commodities to consumer goods, includes a range of intermediate players such as wholesalers, financers, insurers, transporters, and warehousers. These middlemen reduce transaction costs for functions that are outside the firm; that is, they mediate between the firm and the customer. Middlemen are valuable to the transaction only if they are cheaper than the equivalent functions found on the open market. Consequently, it's no surprise that as technology reduces transaction costs in the open market, the role of middleman is coming under attack and the power dynamic among the players is changing rapidly. If buyers and sellers can find each other cheaply over the Internet, who needs agents (for instance, insurance) and distributors (for instance, home computers)? Complex transactions are becoming disaggregated, and middlemen who are not adding sufficient

FIGURE 2.1

Average Cost per Transaction in Retail Banking

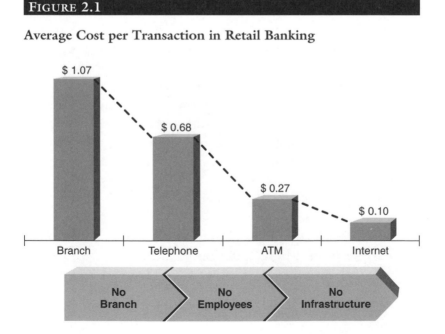

value relative to the open market are being disintermediated, which is to say they're being cut out.

If Auto-by-Tel can leverage itself into a large-scale operation, think of the disruption it will cause to the industry model of the new and used car markets. Manufacturers, dealers, newspapers, insurers, and financers will all find themselves wondering what happened. Even renegade middlemen like Charles Schwab & Co., a leader in the disintermediation of high-price investment firms for small investors, now find themselves threatened by even cheaper technology solutions over the Web (e.g., E*Trade, which operates solely in cyberspace). A cartel of optometrists that controlled the lucrative market for contact lenses is being broken up by the superior technology of drugstores, mail order companies, and Web businesses such as Lens 4 Me Web.

Outsourcing and Downsizing

As transaction costs fall, many organizations have already farmed out functions like purchasing, travel, data processing, and accounting to outsource partners that can operate, thanks in large part to new digital technology, on scale. Despite admonitions to focus on the organization's "core competence" (those activities the firm does particularly better inside than outside), firms today don't usually decide on their own to outsource a function that's no longer efficiently performed inside; rather, the outsourcer comes to them with the economics already worked out. To return to our paper clip example, many firms have already adopted an intermediate solution of turning supplies, copying, and other purely administrative activities over to outsource partners, who often actually reemploy the firm's employees who formerly performed the function but now operate it as a profitable business.

Even when the former employees aren't retained, the rush to outsource explains why, despite continual and massive downsizing in nearly every industry, the unemployment rate in the

United States is near record lows (it is high in much of Europe, but this seems more a function of overregulation and the upheavals being caused by the collapse of Communism in Eastern Europe and the shift to European Union than to downsizing). It's not that people are losing their jobs, it's that they are increasingly shifting from large firms to smaller ones. Just as the Law of Diminishing Firms suggests, the U.S. Department of Labor is already predicting that by the year 2005 the largest employer in the country will be "self."

Outsourcing and downsizing are part of the transition to the new digital economy, in effect replacing monolithic, General Motors-style firms with smaller, more specialized players who, as we'll see, are tied together not by ownership (and bureaucracy) but by high bandwidth data and communication links. How far will this go? Consider two examples. Mastercard, which processes millions of credit card transactions a day, has only 1,000 employees, 800 of them in data processing; Sara Lee recently announced plans to sell off most of its manufacturing assets, leaving it free to concentrate on managing its brands.

Bits as Public Goods

A second critical feature of the old economics that takes on new meaning in the world of killer apps has to do with the properties of information as a good. Computer hackers chant that "information should be free." The notion that we should give away our valuable property sounds at best irrational, and yet, when that "property" is information, economists have understood the value of doing so at least since the time of Adam Smith. Information is part of a special class of commodities that economists refer to as public goods. Where traditional goods like crops, minerals, and cars can be owned and used by only one person at a time, public goods (e.g., national defense and lighthouses) can be owned and used by everyone simultaneously. Since sharing them with as many people as possible spreads their value without adding to their production costs, the goal for a producer is to find a way to pay for their development without invoking the pricing system of supply and demand, which works best for traditional goods.

Laws that grant copyrights and patents to writers and inventors for their work are aimed at exploiting the public goods nature of information and suggest how an economy for bits might best operate. These laws grant a monopoly the author can use to maximize the value of his or her investment. While copyright and patent might be thought of as contrary to the idea of a public good, remember that the monopoly granted is a limited one—in the United States the owner of a copyright holds it only for his or her lifetime plus fifty years, and patents are good only for seventeen years. After this period, the work or the invention (including the information necessary to re-create it) goes into the public domain, where it stays forever. Moreover, copyright applies only to the author's *actual words*—the ideas in a work, like this book, go into the public domain immediately. Motorola recently won a case in which the National Basketball Association claimed that Motorola's sports paging device violated the association's copyright in the broadcast of basketball games. Not so, said the court. Scores—even interim scores—are public information. Everyone can use them, any way they like.

Intellectual property rights are granted solely to encourage the creation of useful information ("To promote the Progress of Science and the useful Arts," as the U.S. Constitution puts it), and the trick has always been to strike the right balance between incentives for creators and the value the public derives from unlimited access and use. It's a balance that is being actively reconsidered in light of the ease with which information in the form of bits can be spread over public networks like the Internet. Many observers (including the authors), believe that large entertainment and publishing companies are trying to shift it in precisely the wrong direction.

Information, like other public goods, is inexhaustible, but information has an additional property that is unique. Information actually *increases in value* the more people use it, one reason why we think less, not more, protection would benefit everyone, including the owners of copyrights. The latest John

Grisham novel—the content, not the actual physical copy we call a book—is a public good in this sense. Everyone can read it at the same time, and the fact that everyone is reading it means that everyone knows what Grisham thinks about the practice of law or the criminal justice system. This collective knowledge creates a context for discussion about these ideas and about Grisham's skills as a storyteller, a phenomenon that becomes increasingly powerful once a critical mass of people have read the novel.

If and when novels can be distributed with little cost over the Internet, a new author might be well served to give away his or her first book to as many people as possible. This would create a ready market for the next book. The cost of the give-away would be much less than in today's publishing business, where the price of a book reflects the author's and publisher's intellectual investment only to a small degree, while the majority of the cost reflects the creation, transportation, and retailing of the physical artifact. Giving away the bits creates a network, and networks, as we noted in Chapter 1, are powerful generators of value. Information increases in value as it is used, the economic expression of Metcalfe's Law. As the Electronic Frontier Foundation's John Perry Barlow said insightfully in rewriting the hacker motto, "Information *wants* to be free."

The New Firm: Rebuilding with Bits

If the Law of Diminishing Firms explains the disruption to current business, the public goods aspect of information accounts for the phenomenal opportunities for growth that are emerging at the same time. Because information wants to be free, the sudden creation of cyberspace, a viable home for free-moving bits, is driving a massive information migration. During 1997, Inter-NIC, the company responsible for registering site names on the World Wide Web, reported that new sites were being added at the rate of one every minute. Libraries, publishers, financial service firms, and buyers and sellers of every kind have been flooding cyberspace with their information archives. Some of Wall

Street's hottest technology stocks are for companies like Yahoo!, Excite, and Alta Vista, all of which simply help users to navigate through this amazing wealth of knowledge.

Just as cheap bits are shrinking the traditional firm, their public goods features are building firms back up again, using bits for the bricks and mortar. The new forms, however, look little like their predecessors. As information flow increases, organizations are less able to hide their costs and pass along inefficiencies to customers. So they must focus, as authors Gary Hamel and C. K. Prahalad argue in *Competing for the Future,* on those activities that truly add value; that is, activities they can perform, owing to their expertise, scale, and other special properties, more efficiently than everyone else. Companies already struggling with these changes have found that the first wave of displacement involves employees. But people can be retrained. The next phase of restructuring is more difficult. Fixed assets—the trucks, pieces of manufacturing equipment, factories, and warehouses that were a necessary evil of running an integrated firm—are not so flexible.

New entrants and early adopters of new technologies do not have fixed assets, and in the new economy, what was an advantage will quickly become a disadvantage. Digital publishers don't have or need printing presses, a distribution network, and retailer contracts. Digital insurance firms and banks don't have or need agents and branches. And digital shopping malls don't need any of the three key assets of traditional retailers: location, location, and location. New digital competitors can still reach an exploding, global, unregulated market overnight, and at very little start-up cost. The barriers to competition are falling fast, falling at the speed of a bit. Software giant Microsoft is already offering services as varied as event ticket sales, travel reservations, home and car shopping, and investment advice.

In effect, someone has just turned your balance sheet upside down. As the CEO of a leading durable goods manufacturer told us, "The leverage has shifted to the consumer. They know when they're getting value and when they're not getting value and will pay for service where there is quality service. If there is no value added to high-cost distribution systems, they aren't going to pay for them." Utilities, used to passing along cost overruns from plants they didn't need to build directly to consumers, have a new term to describe these items in a deregulated environment. They call them "stranded assets."

Getting caught with stranded assets, even ones that you considered just the other day to be the source of your competitive advantage, isn't hard. It can happen with remarkable speed, even in markets that aren't highly regulated. In the early 1990s, Microsoft's Bill Gates approached Encyclopedia Britannica about creating a digital version of its leading encyclopedia, to be delivered on the increasingly cheap medium of CD-ROM. Britannica, concerned that licensing content would jeopardize the high margin market for their printed books, turned him down. So Gates created his own encyclopedia, Encarta, using content from Funk and Wagnalls and public domain audio and visuals. From the beginning, Encarta was published exclusively in digital form. Not only is the multimedia product more engaging than the cold text, it is cheaper to produce and distribute ($1.50 to press the CD-ROM versus $250 to print the book), and easily updated as well.

Within eighteen months, Microsoft Encarta became the best-selling encyclopedia in the world. Britannica saw its own market collapse. Britannica approached Gates about reconsidering his deal. The meeting ended, according to Gates, when he informed the company that his market research showed that the Britannica brand name now had negative value in the new interactive encyclopedia market and that the company would need to pay *him* to use its name on *his* product. Since then, Britannica has changed hands several times, eliminated its direct sales force, and struggled to gain market share with a competing CD-ROM product, initially priced at $1,000.

Information Assets

The good news is that there's a new item in the asset column, one you're probably not even accounting for: your information assets. These include everything from expertise, trademarks,

market intelligence, goodwill, and processes to corporate culture and identity, most of which are today considered too soft to
include in a company balance sheet (accountants are likely to
suffer from the Law of Disruption). Information assets will for
many organizations become goods and services themselves,
subject to the economic rules of public goods.

Many organizations have already recognized the power of
information assets. Some are even willing to put a value on
them. Jewel grocery stores give their customers a "Preferred
Card" that allows the stores to capture and market perfect sales
data, connecting customers with the complete details of what
and when they buy. Jewel compensates the customers for cooperating in the collection of this information by providing discounts on various products only to customers who use their
Preferred Card.

One start-up company is at work developing tools specifically
for consolidating and distributing information assets. The company, Digital Knowledge Assets, works with business school
professors to translate as much of their classroom experience as
possible into digital form, hoping to distribute it more widely to
a corporate audience that can't physically attend classes. But the
toolset they are developing, which includes virtual "tours" of
case study companies and software that sorts and selects news
items of interest based on a set of common criteria, is equally
useful inside a company. DKA's first customer was a large electronics manufacturer that was more interested in the tools and
DKA's expertise in information design than outside content.
Their second customer was a consulting firm.

Our clients frequently challenge us to find information assets
hiding in their organization. Doing so never takes long. Distributors have logistics, manufacturers have engineering, retailers
have customers. Valuable information surrounds each of these
functions. Invariably, the information assets we find aren't in a
usable form, since they're spread over numerous departments
and information systems, many of them not even automated. As
Moore's Law makes processing power and data storage un-
speakably cheap, the cost of collecting and consolidating these
disparate data becomes less of an obstacle. Still, learning to

exploit these assets will take imagination. Already, media companies including publishers Simon & Schuster and Time Warner are hurrying to produce "corporate digital archives" of their text, photo, and promotional materials. These organizations are first because they have to be—their businesses depend on the reusability of content. But so do yours, sooner or later.

To identify your own information assets, start with activities that already contain components of public goods, such as marketing and advertising. The goal of advertising is to spread knowledge about the company's goods and services to as wide an audience as possible, an example of a current practice of giving information away to increase its value. Once a critical mass of people know about the product, they act as a source of credibility, which can be expressed in shorthand as a brand or product name and communicated in the form of trademarks. The logos for Coca-Cola, McDonald's, and Nike are valuable because they are universally recognized and because the associations with them are consistent and predictable.

Everything you move from the world of atoms to the world of bits will be a kind of public good, behaving the way brands and trademarks do today. Today your logo may be your primary public good, but tomorrow it may be supplemented by your inventory, your money, your business partnerships, and your production schedule. As technologies for large-scale collaboration that creates a virtual workspace for scattered project teams become cost effective, the information assets of development projects shift into public goods. Instead of involving customers and suppliers in the design and testing of new goods and services as you may do today, you may find yourself following the lead of product innovation specialist Hewlett-Packard, which, in effect, outsources much of this work to its business partners. By doing so you start to build a network for developing new products before the current products are even finished.

The more functions you can express as information and translate into bits, the more you can take advantage of the Metcalfe effect. As the information elements of manufacturing, distribution, and other processes become digital, in fact, the bright lines between these activities turn out to be largely a function of their physical nature. Marketing, recruiting, training, investor relations, and even manufacturing are already merging for strong international brands like McDonald's, where a computer game to optimize the production of hamburgers, given away as a premium, might serve all five activities. We believe that in the new economy many traditional functions merge into one overall activity. For the moment, let's call that one activity what it is today: brand management.

Part 2 describes some strategies for profiting from this feature of the new economy. But consider for now that brand management today is more than likely a separate and highly specialized activity in your organization, usually managed by experts. Tomorrow, it may be a skill that everyone will need.

Old Coase, New Coase; Old Public Goods, New Public Goods

Today's killer apps, operating under Moore's Law and Metcalfe's Law, are expressing their disruption potential on today's business models by changing the economic rules of the game. As it turns out, the principles that animate this new economy—Coase's theory of transaction costs and the concept of public goods—have been known for decades or longer. Now they take center stage.

In the new economy, the balance of activity between firms and the market, between middlemen and the buyers and suppliers they sit between, changes dramatically. Early exploiters of new technology disrupt value chains, cartels, industry structures, and the delicate balances between sellers and customers, between regulators and the regulated, and partners and competitors. New rules and new structures will rise and fall with increasing velocity, new operating models and new competitors will come and go, and activities will morph into others or disappear altogether.

The rapid reduction in transaction costs in the open market has caught traditional industrial-age organizations by surprise, especially those sheltered from market competitors by regulation or cartel. These firms must now find new ways to offer and communicate their value. The power of information as a public good, both its inexhaustibility and its ability to increase in value through use, has launched a massive shift of information, much of it once considered proprietary, to cyberspace. Those who are first to embrace and exploit the powerful but unfamiliar features of public goods can gain significant advantage over organizations that still treat their information assets as they would gold bars or manufacturing processes; that is, by hoarding them.

This is a brave new world—one that requires a new strategy. In the age of digital killer apps, it requires a digital strategy.

3

digital strategy

The best way to predict the future is to invent it.
—Alan Kay

IF CYBERSPACE is the new business environment, Moore's Law describes the behavior of its most basic elements, while Metcalfe's Law describes how you can create a kind of chain reaction between them. Coasean and public goods economics provide the basic rules of survival: the lowest transaction costs prevail; new wealth is created by mining information assets. Killer apps are the results of these principles operating together.

Now that you understand the basic problem, what are you going to do about it? Nearly every executive we have spoken to in the last two years recognizes that they must do *something*. Perhaps, like many of our clients, you are already trying to make sense of the digital age and formulate a strategic response. To respond to changed circumstances, clients often dust off the old strategic plan, identify which assumptions have changed, and try to adjust the plan accordingly.

This response will get you only part of the way there—in any event, not far enough. What we do is take strategic planning as the starting point and work with clients to see how both the tools and processes must be altered to function in the new environment. Radical change is the order of the day. It isn't only the planning assumptions—a new competitor, perhaps, or a decision to expand the operation overseas—that have changed. What has changed in addition are the basic principles underlying *how* you develop products, operate, and yes, even plan. To succeed digitally, you need to eat, sleep, breathe, and think digitally.

It can be done, and not just by companies like Microsoft or the latest Internet start-up, companies whose actual goods and services are already digital. Our clients have included a major fast-food franchiser, an integrated oil and gas giant, a large European conglomerate, and even the British Post Office. Like astronauts learning to perform basic tasks in zero gravity, the executives in these decidedly undigital companies find the first few times through are hard going, but after that the process comes much easier.

We have developed a new approach to strategic planning, which we call *digital strategy*. Digital strategy consists of twelve design principles that guide the process for finding and shaping killer apps, and techniques that organizations of any size and in any industry can use to achieve market dominance. The design principles are described in Part 2 of this book; Part 3 provides examples of how organizations have made the transition to the new operating model.

In this chapter, we describe the key differences between digital strategy and today's approach to planning, a model that has dominated for the last twenty years. It doesn't matter if your organization doesn't do strategic planning now, or if you aren't yourself directly involved. In the new business environment, as the story of Chris Brennan and the BP kiosk demonstrates, managers (and everyone else) are the strategists. This means you need to understand how the basic approach works. You also need to recognize the many pitfalls of traditional strategy that you should avoid. Table 3.1 summarizes the key differences.

The Rise and Fall of Strategic Planning

Michael Porter's *Competitive Advantage,* published in 1980, is the classic statement of traditional strategic planning. Porter argues that sustaining above-average performance requires a strategy and the will to implement it. His book explains how to analyze market conditions, assess competitive strengths and weaknesses, and develop long-term strategies for keeping a competitive edge, as well as how to monitor the progress of those strategies.

While many of Porter's techniques are still salutary, we believe they are largely unsuitable to life in cyberspace. Porter implicitly recognized this himself in a 1996 *Harvard Business Review* article in which he criticized the failure of most executives

TABLE 3.1

Strategic Planning versus Digital Strategy

	Strategic Planning	*Digital Strategy*
Nature	Static	Dynamic
Environment	Physical	Virtual
Discipline	Analytical	Intuitive
Time Frame	3–5 years	12–18 months
Key Pressure Point	Five forces	New forces
Key Technique	Value chain leverage	Value chain destruction
Participants	Strategists, senior management	Everyone (including business partners)
Technology's Role	Enabler	Disrupter
Output	Plan	Killer apps

to follow his original advice, a failure he blamed on distractions like business process reengineering, total quality management, and a host of avoidance behaviors like preparing mission statements and corporate visions that masquerade as strategy. (Cartoonist Scott Adams makes a similar point, with an acid tongue, in *The Dilbert Principle*.)

Porter concedes that "developing a strategy in a newly emerging industry or in a business undergoing revolutionary technological change is a daunting proposition." He just doesn't believe that most industries have or will soon enter "a new era of competition," in which, owing to digital technology, "none of the old rules are valid." He believes, in other words, in clean lines separating industries and competitors from each other and stable markets in which companies can experiment with new goods or services. In Porter's view, the relationships between the major players in any given industry are largely fixed.

It is here that we part company with Porter. Every industry we can think of is already in the midst of "revolutionary technological change," and will be for at least as long as Moore's Law holds. Though the primary technology of industries like transportation, oil exploration, and manufacturing may be relatively stable, industries whose primary product or service is or includes information, such as entertainment, retailing, financial services, and chemicals, are involved in major technological shifts.

More to the point, *every* industry is going through a revolution in its use of information technology. In transportation today, logistics is the key to the leverage exploited by package deliverers like FedEx and UPS; carriers of larger sized loads are trapped in a commodity-priced market. In retail, databases and computer networks allow customers to find out quickly and easily who has what they need, when they'll have it, and how much it really costs them to produce and deliver it. The information component of every business transaction is significant, if not dominant. As digital technology reduces the transaction cost of collecting and exploiting that information, seismic shifts between the participants occur.

Traditional planning simply doesn't work in times of great change. Henry Mintzberg, in his 1994 book entitled *The Rise and Fall of Strategic Planning,* argues that one of traditional strategic planning's false assumptions generally is that the future can be forecast based on current climatic conditions in the business environment. Part of the problem, he says, is that "discontinuities" like technological innovations make forecasting practically impossible. And discontinuity, as the Law of Disruption suggests, is the primary characteristic of the new business environment. The current batch of killer apps, including the global computing network, inexpensive high-speed data transmission and storage, and a revolution in new software interfaces, is sending shock waves into the information component of every industry. The effects cannot be easily predicted or systematically addressed—not, in any case, by the traditional methods of planning.

The Practice of Digital Strategy

Digital strategy, as Table 3.1 suggests, departs in many key respects from traditional strategy work. The foremost difference is the role played by technology itself. In our work as consultants, we confess to having preached a dogma that has since become heresy in the new world. In developing large-scale information systems with Andersen Consulting, participating in corporate strategy projects with McKinsey & Co., and working on massive reengineering projects as part of CSC Index, we treated digital technology as the critical tool for implementing change. Our project teams would decide how the business should change and then would throw the new model over to the Information Services (I/S) department, which was expected to design the systems components of the new solution. I/S was rarely included in the process of forming the business solution. Technology, as Michael Hammer and James Champy wrote in *Reengineering the Corporation,* was the "essential enabler" of change.

This attitude toward technology is wrong today and will be wrong in the conceivable future. Business change now *originates* with digital technology, in particular with the killer apps. Executives from every department must learn that in the new world technology has become and will remain the *essential disrupter* of current operating models and their underlying assumptions. Technology, as we've said, isn't the solution. It's the problem.

There are more subtle differences between the old and new approaches. In traditional strategy, the plan produced is largely static. A team goes off for a period of time, performs its analysis, and returns with a document (often bound as a book), which remains the plan until the next planning cycle. In theory, this book predicts the future well enough to serve as a guide for the organization's key decision-makers; but in practice the plan is rarely referenced, and then only to chill unplanned innovative thinking that might escape from the field organization. The team is generally made up of senior executives, or the staff of a specialized department devoted full-time to strategy and corporate planning.

This is not the case with digital strategy. A digital strategy is at its core a dynamic plan, one that requires not just regular but constant rethinking. The responsibility for questioning the strategy is not the specialized task of a single person or department, but is open to everyone, particularly line managers in large organizations or functional heads in smaller ones. The accelerated change of the new business environment is best observed, in our experience, by people on the line who see competitors, meet with customers, and negotiate with suppliers, regulators, and shareholders. These are also the people who, given a chance, will produce the best ideas. As Disney Fellow Alan Kay says, "Context is worth 50 IQ points." Context comes from listening and observing, and that is what managers need to do.

Time Frame

The time frame for traditional strategy work, in practice, is three to five years, though it is increasingly rare to find organizations that are comfortable with the high end of that range. Even three years is too long. Thanks to Moore's Law and Metcalfe's Law, killer apps are entering the bloodstream of commerce quickly and in many cases reach critical mass—the knee of the Metcalfe curve—in less than two years. Executives in industries as varied as education, advertising, government, pharmaceuticals, consumer products, retail, and wholesale tell us that their basic assumptions about products, channels, and customers will be completely changed by digital technology in the next two years, perhaps more than once—even if they don't know exactly how.

Electronic commerce, for example, wasn't part of anyone's strategic plan (not even Microsoft's) two years ago, but it is already a force in nearly every industry. Networking giant Cisco Systems has already moved credit checking, production scheduling, customer support, and other functions to the Web. The company claims a cost savings of $535 million for the first year.

The new planning horizon is now closer to twelve to eighteen months and, as Moore's Law continues its exponential journey, is a vanishing horizon at that. This acceleration means less time to respond and, therefore, less time for analysis or detailed planning. Managers, executives, and entrepreneurs we have worked with increasingly embrace the prospect of implementing strategy well before it is entirely thought out, or before a detailed business case can be developed, in part because of the shrinking window of opportunity. In addition, the new technologies themselves have made it possible to experiment cheaply.

Playboy Enterprises CEO Christie Hefner told us she simply had "an instinctive feeling" that it was time for Playboy to experiment with electronic distribution of its content. The Playboy brand was too valuable, she knew, to cede control to a commercial on-line service like AOL or CompuServe, even though these services had superior technical knowledge and an established customer base. So Playboy launched its own photo archive, initially giving away digital photographs (at a manufacturing and distribution cost of nothing) on the unproven World Wide Web. Hefner had a hunch that something interesting would develop.

It did. The site was so successful—5 million visits a day in 1996—that Playboy was soon able to sell enough advertising to pay the full costs of running the experiment. The site has been redesigned many times, adding and subtracting features as Web technology evolves. Playboy is now offering a subscription-based service, something Hefner avoided doing until technology became available that allowed subscribers to retain anonymity. Hefner is now evaluating new "watermarking" technology, hoping to minimize unauthorized redistribution.

Planning for quick execution begins to lose the appearance of a traditional plan. Instead it resembles more the design of a series of small experiments. For companies operating today in cyberspace, the plan disappears, replaced by a constant tweaking of existing projects and a vigorous marketplace of ideas where new ideas can be floated, argued, and selected or rejected. It is again digital technology that makes these compressed time frames possible.

The New Forces

Sustainable competitive advantage, Porter wrote, requires leverage over at least one of the "Five Forces": our customers, suppliers, competitors, new entrants, and substitutes. The strategy of a cost cutter like Wal-Mart was to establish such significant presence that suppliers are forced to give up margin. For a premium provider, like FedEx, the idea was to offer such unique and valuable services (guaranteed next day delivery and convenient pickups) that customers were willing to pay premium prices. Competitive advantage is whatever strategy a company has to maintain such leverage. Wal-Mart's sheer size makes it difficult for more specialized department stores to duplicate its approach, as these stores have learned to their near destruction. FedEx, as with most "premium" strategists, continually invests in technology to improve their already excellent service.

Achieving competitive advantage was already hard. Now it's even harder. Surrounding the five forces are three new forces: digitization, globalization, and deregulation (see Figure 3.1). These forces, generated by the interaction of digital technology and Coasean economics, exert tremendous new pressure on the competitive environment, superseding the old forces as the focus of planning.

Digitization

As discussed in detail in Chapters 1 and 2, computing power and communications bandwidth, thanks to Moore's Law, are becoming cheap enough to treat as disposable. As costs come down, competitors and the market in general force organizations to move information-intensive activities not only to computer systems but to increasingly public networks, open databases, and collaborative environments, where the new economics multiplies their value. In doing so, traditional business principles

FIGURE 3.1

The New Forces

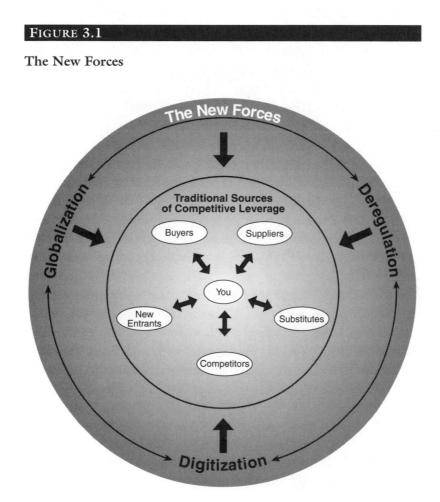

and industry rules are suddenly brought to light. They soon dis-integrate, leading to a period of chaos followed by the rise of new, but less stable, relationships.

Globalization

The world can be thought of as a very large network, and as Met-calfe's Law has shown us, the attraction of such a network is irre-sistible. Improvements in transportation and communications have taken many businesses long considered local to global status, sometimes overnight. In capital markets, for example, globaliza-tion is old news, acknowledged as long ago as 1974, when the United States permanently abandoned the gold standard and chose instead to allow its currency to float with the international market. Today, trillions of units of currency are traded electroni-cally every day. National banks are unable to have an impact on exchange rates even when they want to intervene.

The impact of globalization is felt throughout the produc-tion and distribution life cycle. In upstream activities, it is now common to have component sourcing and assembly provided by a global network of partners and suppliers. For time-sensitive processes, industries as varied as manufacturing and finance take advantage of the earth's rotation by passing work back and forth between Asia, Europe, and the Americas, engaging in 24-hour operation.

Downstream, customers are already used to the idea of bor-derless commerce. Given the chance, they are more than willing to shop on an international basis for everything from entertain-ment to software to cars and electronics, and even for many goods and services traditionally considered national or even local.

Deregulation

Regulation exists in some form for every industry. It often begins as an attempt to restore consumer leverage to markets where, because of scope or monopoly conditions, Adam Smith's "invisible hand" of supply and demand appears not to be operating to regulate price. Such regulations, and the bodies responsible for them, are often captured by the industries they are regulating and become a tool for reducing competition and freezing out new entrants—the very opposite of their objective.

The move for deregulation is generally stimulated by a wide-spread belief of buyers and sellers that the cure has become worse than the disease, a recognition that the free market, thanks to plunging transaction costs, is now the better regulator of an industry than government. Sometimes, as in the case of U.S. railroads earlier this century and banking today, deregulation follows a realization that some substitute has become available from an unregulated set of providers, making it difficult, if not impossible, for the regulated players to compete.

The current mania for deregulation, evident in everything from the airline, communications, utilities and banking industries in the United States and Europe, the passage of GATT and NAFTA, the dramatic development of the European Union and the even more dramatic collapse of the highly regulated economies of the former Soviet republics, might be grossly simplified as an expression of the Law of Diminishing Firms. Regulated markets, like firms, are nonmarket solutions aimed at reducing the transaction costs of a variety of activities. Like firms, regulated industries do not avoid all the costs but try to replace market costs with a set of cheaper alternatives. When they do not, pressure builds to deregulate.

In international telephone calling, for example, regulated prices encouraged the rise of companies that used technologies like leased data lines, satellites, and automated callback systems to circumvent local monopolies. The success of these companies encouraged the national telcos to sign a pact in early 1997 to open markets and reduce inter-company charges. Deregulation will spur additional competition and the development of more technology. The net result is that consumers will save as much as a trillion dollars over the next 10 to 12 years.

The Forces in Operation

Impressive enough on their own, the new forces in operation interact with each other, so much so that they begin to look like one and the same thing. Together, they are an overwhelming and disruptive influence everyone senses but no one can see. Digital technologies make it possible to manage a wider variety of relationships with buyers and suppliers, which feeds globalization. The more global the economy becomes, the more local regulations tend to hold back the industries they were written to protect, increasing the velocity of deregulation. Deregulation opens previously closed markets to competition, exposing chronic underinvestment in technology. Then the whole cycle starts over again.

In commercial banking, the industry itself spearheaded efforts to ease regulations that limited the use of technologies, including ATMs, telephone banking, and now Internet banking, each of which has been introduced to improve costs. Inadvertently, these applications also opened banks to new competitors, like network operators and software providers, that can extract value from high-volume transaction processing. The technology also revealed how little customers actually value in-person branch banking.

In 1995 Security First Network Bank became the first entirely virtual bank, operating solely on the Internet. Its customers pay minimum fees but have the convenience of tellerless banking anytime and anywhere. Thanks to the regulatory structure still in place, bank deposits at Security First are insured by the U.S. government and are therefore as secure as they would be at a traditional bank. Security First could not have come into existence without the deregulation traditional banks lobbied for to enable their own use of technology. But Security First has used the same technology as a threat. Even though Wells Fargo, as noted in Chapter 2, uses the Internet and other digital technologies to reduce the number of branches it operates, Security First has no branches whatsoever. Its infrastructure costs are insignificant compared with those of Wells Fargo, even after the consolidation that followed Wells Fargo's merger with First Interstate.

Companies like Intuit and Microsoft, as well as brokerage firms and insurance companies, go further still, offering banking-like functions from outside the regulated environment. These providers have the cost advantage of Security First as well as flexibility that banks lack. Banks, eager to expand into other services to compete with these nonbanks, find themselves restricted by regulations aimed at minimizing competition. Their attempts to control deregulation for their own advantage seem likely to have done just the opposite, creating a panic in the industry to deregulate, globalize, and digitize even faster.

Caution: Value Chains under Extreme Pressure

Traditional strategy is implemented through what Michael Porter calls the *value chain*. The value chain is the set of activities an organization performs to create and distribute its goods and services, including direct activities like procurement and production and indirect activities like human resources and finance. Each of these activities adds some value to the product, a value that Porter refers to as "margin." The more competitive the value chain of the organization, the more the overall product's value exceeds the sum of its parts, and hence the more margin the firm can realize as profits.

Competitive advantage is achieved when an organization links the activities in its value chain more cheaply or more expertly than do its competitors. Professor Mintzberg is skeptical that an organization can ever truly execute such a plan. Strategy can succeed, he wrote, only if "[w]hile the planning is done, and historical data are analyzed, the world sits patiently by."

If there ever was a time when the world could be counted on to hold still, it is long over. Today, even organizations that produce physical goods have value chains that are information intensive (marketing, sales, service, and much of the production function itself, for example). For service organizations, the product itself is information or information based. The new forces are wreaking havoc on value chains of even superior companies. In industries as varied as banking, insurance, and utilities, competitive advantage is being wiped out as new, sometimes bizarre, competitors quickly produce new value chains that use digital technology to alter the equation radically. To respond effectively, organizations must now consider scrapping, rather than optimizing, their value chains.

The chief executive of a large greeting card company, for instance, told us that he believes the Internet will increase sales because customers will be able to act more easily on impulse, buying greetings whenever and wherever they want. Greetings may also be sent electronically at the last minute and still arrive on time. The company may even send a reminder by E-mail to the customer based on a list of important dates provided up front. But at the same time, he recognizes that the Internet creates a cheap global distribution channel that new competitors can use to sell greetings, turning the printing presses and physical locations of his distributors from assets into liabilities.

Given these forces, the company's strategy can no longer be based on tinkering with today's value chain. Instead, the CEO must find ways to alter it dramatically, if not destroy it altogether. The company might, for example, recognize its content, rather than its distribution network, as the chief asset. The archived material and the company's expertise in bringing creative people together to create a wide range of sentiments might in this scenario be the basis for a new incarnation of the company as a service provider rather than a retailer. The company might, in other words, offer highly customized or even one-of-a-kind greetings for any type of occasion, helping consumers express their feelings almost as a counselor would. In the interim, the company can begin to wean itself off the physical assets before others realize how quickly they are depreciating.

In the United Kingdom, Barclays Bank has launched an electronic shopping mall, BarclaySquare, to give the merchant customers of its credit card business a quick and powerful entry point into electronic commerce. BarclaySquare consists of electronic catalogs for academic bookseller Blackwell's, wine merchant J. Sainsbury, and others, and offers electronic reservations and ticketing for the EuroStar train. Transactions are backed by the solid reputation of a stately English bank.

Compare the value chain of Barclays with that of a traditional shopping mall developer and you find very little in common. The developer's key asset (and cost) is real estate, and it derives margin primarily from rent. The actual cost of construction and operation of the electronic mall, on the other hand, is trivial, and Barclays makes money as a percentage of credit card transactions it clears on behalf of its "tenants," just as it does in nonelectronic transactions. Barclays created its mall solely to increase the volume of transactions of its merchant customers, but in doing so it linked the incentives for mall operator and retailer in a way that doesn't exist in the physical mall, or at least not to the same extent.

How does the shopping mall developer, a real estate company, compete with a bank that has none of its operating costs and a very different set of financial incentives? What happens when the mall's competitive advantage, based almost entirely on location, is turned against it by a new competitor that lets consumers shop from any location in the world at any time of day or night? Three years after BarclaySquare opened its doors, is there a shopping mall developer in the world who recognizes the bank as a competitor, let alone a competitive threat?

As this example suggests, BarlaySquare and other electronic malls have the potential to destroy the value chains of a variety of today's retail firms. Shopping mall developers are an obvious target, but so too are subsidiary industries like advertising, construction, customer service, and distributors. Barclays is not just a new competitor, but the creator of an entirely new way of deriving revenue. If it is successful, BarclaySquare will erase competitive advantage for companies far removed from its own sphere of activity. And its development is being led, not enabled, by digital technology.

Strategy's Dirty Little Secret

Gary Hamel wrote in a 1997 *Fortune* cover story that the "dirty little secret" of the strategy industry, of which he is a leading practitioner, is that it "doesn't have any theory of strategy creation." The truly innovative strategies, he says, "are always, and I mean always, the result of lucky foresight." Digital strategy is a radical new approach to strategic planning, one that doesn't pretend to create strategies so much as to create an environment where lucky foresight is more likely to make an appearance. It shares few features with traditional strategy development and deployment techniques. It values creativity and intuition. Its development is not the task of a few individuals, but of an entire organization, communicating on as open and wide a channel as technology will permit. Most of all, it recognizes technology not as a tool for implementing a static strategy but as a constant disrupter creating both threats and opportunities that wide-awake organizations can turn into killer apps for their own benefit.

The techniques of digital strategy are being developed by companies around the world today as they experiment with digital technologies and attempt to let loose their own killer apps. From our participation in these efforts, and from studying both winning and losing examples, we have gleaned a few rules of thumb that can help you develop a digital strategy of your own. These rules are the subject of Part 2.

designing the
killer app

TECHNOLOGY IS NOW the central driver of the business economy. Cyberspace may already be the home office of every global enterprise. As we demonstrated in Part 1, the rapid appearance and strange economic behavior of the latest generation of digital technologies has created a new world in which many of the old rules don't apply. Today's tools for setting and executing strategy turn out to be artifacts of the industrial age that spawned them, and likewise don't work in the new climate.

This part of the book describes twelve new rules for designing killer apps of your own. We have organized these rules into three stages, analogous to the major tasks of any complex problem of design: reshaping the landscape, building new connections, and redefining the interior (see Figure 2.A).

The first stage of designing any structure is to identify and evaluate an appropriate site. At a minimum, this requires an understanding of the environment and its constraints, including natural limits like soil, weather, danger of earthquake and other disasters, and of manmade features such as traffic patterns, zoning, noise, and pollution. These determine the nature and scale of the structure you can build. You must also understand the build-

FIGURE 2.A

The Three Stages of Killer App Design

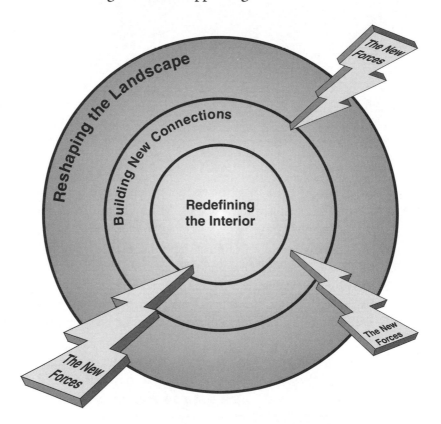

ings around your site, to fit in and at the same time to distinguish yourself.

In cyberspace, the new business environment is largely defined by the organizations and individuals with whom you interact, what we have earlier referred to as business partners. Most organizations are comfortable thinking about strategy in terms of interactions with customers, suppliers, and competitors, but in digital strategy the category is much broader. The range of relationships is also broad, going far beyond simple categories like buyer and seller, or supplier and producer. Chapter 4 presents new rules for dealing with the outside environment through interactions with customers and other business partners. These rules emphasize the liberating (and threatening) aspects of plummeting transaction costs. They also highlight the value of treating the new business environment as an evolving community, increasingly bound together by cheap digital technology, rather than as a discrete and largely static set of individual actors.

In architecture, the second major task is to design the structure, and in particular the face it presents to the outside world. A building is a set of systems, and the external design represents the interface not only to the occupants but to everyone who comes in contact with it. A good design meets all of the constraints of the site, while a superior design does so in a way that manages to express the character of its function in the architecture itself. Structures like the Eiffel Tower, the Brooklyn Bridge, Hoover Dam, and traditional Japanese homes bind the design to the physical structure so tightly that the two are largely indistinguishable.

Interfaces for killer apps are built in software, a material that is both cheap and highly flexible. In cyberspace, there is little additional cost, relatively speaking, for an interface that looks more like the Taj Mahal than a lean-to. Virtual interfaces can be taken down and redeveloped at will, without the need for scaffolding to cover the old design while the new one is being applied. Chapter 5 describes ways of building interfaces that not only generate dramatic new images for your organization but move much of the interaction between your organization and its business partners into the interface itself. There, everyone benefits from the superior economic behavior of the medium.

The third major task is to rehabilitate the interior of a structure, including preexisting portions, to a new set of uses. Rehabbing within the constraints of both the site and the design improves the performance of the structure and its systems, keeping the building "alive" through generations of environmental and design changes. In many urban centers in the United States, for example, train stations have been reconfigured as shopping malls, warehouses have become premium residences, and abandoned or ignored waterfronts have become parks and community gathering places.

Rehabbing your organization requires a similar degree of ingenuity. Old structures must be torn down and new ones constructed, but always within the organizational culture that serves as the foundation. Rules for managing this transformation are the subject of Chapter 6. As the Law of Diminishing Firms pushes organizations into more temporary and decentralized entities, we demonstrate how the very same technologies that are forcing these changes can be used to create businesses that are modular, always ready to adapt to new demands and new opportunities.

The twelve design principles are the beginning of a building code for commercial organizations in cyberspace (see Table 2.A). For each of the three phases outlined above, we present four such rules. Together, the principles can help you jump-start the development of your own digital strategy. Separately, they are the rules from which you develop your own killer apps.

We also show how the rules follow from the new competitive environment we described in Part 1, the logical result of Moore, Metcalfe, and Coasean economics, operating through the Law of Disruption and the new forces. Connecting the rules to the framework described in Part 1 should help diminish the anxiety you might feel at adopting so counterintuitive a notion as cannibalizing your own market, giving away your most valuable information, or destroying your own value chain. To help further, we provide numerous examples from a wide range of industries and organizations, many of industrial-age vintage, that have proven the rule through their own efforts to develop killer apps.

TABLE 2.A

The Twelve Principles of Killer App Design

Reshaping the Landscape

1. Outsource to the customer.

2. Cannibalize your markets.

3. Treat each customer as a market segment of one.

4. Create communities of value.

Building New Connections

5. Replace rude interfaces with learning interfaces.

6. Ensure continuity for the customer, not yourself.

7. Give away as much information as you can.

8. Structure every transaction as a joint venture.

Redefining the Interior

9. Treat your assets as liabilities.

10. Destroy your value chain.

11. Manage innovation as a portfolio of options.

12. Hire the children.

4

reshaping the landscape

You cannot plan out a new form of society in advance, then set it up and expect it to function as it was designed to.
—The Unabomber Manifesto

As long as you depend on the statistical aggregates we now call information, you'll know a good deal about your product, a good deal about your services, and not a blessed thing about your customers.
—Peter Drucker

RELATIONSHIPS WITH the outside environment, or in other words, your business partners, are already under profound pressure from the new forces. The most obvious symptom of this pressure is the shifting definition of what is inside and what is outside of the firm. As the new forces drive down transaction costs, you must continually revisit your own operational model and decide which functions are more efficiently handled by the market—then move them there as quickly as possible. As you do, the remarkable property of information to increase in value the more it is used will lead you to more surprising changes. It turns out, for example, that customers are not only lower-cost providers of many activities we think of today as "customer service," but customers perceive and realize added benefit from doing these tasks themselves.

The disruptive power of technology, on the other hand, exposes you to new and unfamiliar competitors. The decline in technology costs and the value generated by the effects of Metcalfe's Law unintentionally destroy barriers to entry even in markets and industries long thought impenetrable, including traditional "natural" monopolies like telecommunications and other utilities. These and other industries now find themselves being redefined by information brokers who stand to capture a healthy share of the profit margin using the new forces as leverage. To avoid the resulting killer apps you must adopt them yourself, trading off your existing brand and other information assets to ward off the newcomers even as you accelerate the destruction of your own business model.

Lower information costs, moreover, make it possible to think of and measure your daily operations as a series of unique transactions rather than broad categories like products and customer segments. As transaction costs approach zero, in fact, the Law of Diminishing Firms reveals that standard products are nothing more than a brute force approach to reducing the transaction costs of collecting and responding to the needs of individual business partners, an approach that is now unnecessary. As consultant and author Joe Pine puts it, "Anything you can digitize, you can customize."

The migration from atoms to bits is also creating a new importance for relationships that generate value through information exchange. Even as you outsource uneconomical functions to business partners, making the relationship with the outsourced functions more casual, the diversity and bandwidth of other interactions increase dramatically. As we approach (but never reach) the world of truly frictionless transactions, an organization's relationships are optimized by treating them as a community rather than a series of contracts.

Oddly enough, what most enhances your network of relationships is to improve the connections *between* business partners, who have much to say to each other but no forum in which to communicate. Organizations are used to working hard to keep business partners apart, and find it difficult to understand how bringing them together generates new value, much of which they can capture through creative brand management. For organizations that begin life digitally, building themselves by building communities is as natural as breathing.

These first four design principles are examined in this chapter:

1. Outsource to the customer.

2. Cannibalize your markets.

3. Treat each customer as a market segment of one.

4. Create communities of value.

These principles can be used to design killer apps that develop new markets, to form new relationships with customers and other business partners, and to apply digital technology to change the nature of the goods and services you currently offer. Companies that have employed them have found new ways of collecting, consolidating, and valuing information, much of which is freely available and, indeed, may already be resident in their own databases. Customers and others, it turns out, are more than happy to provide the rest.

1. Outsource to the Customer

Most organizations are already familiar with the concept of outsourcing, which we described in Chapter 2 as an expression of Coasean economics at work: as digital technologies make the market more efficient, companies can and indeed must turn over uneconomic functions, including some or all data processing and other office management tasks, to stay competitive. In cyberspace, the economics of information flow create a related opportunity. Data collection and customer service functions can now be outsourced, not to other firms, but directly to the customer. Customers take on these tasks willingly, extracting value of their own by doing them.

You outsource to customers by building an interface into your information sources and then giving customers the tools they need to navigate and customize them. The data is generally already digital and using the Web and its toolset makes it cheap to build, deploy, and operate that interface. The customer connects to your systems using his or her own equipment, phone lines, office space, and even electricity, which means you don't need to provide it any longer.

For a small investment, you can have the customer perform many of the expensive activities you do today, including basic customer service, order entry and tracking, training, purchase order management, product configuration, and even product development. The data you collect has far fewer errors because it has been handled only once, and then by the originating source. Cost savings on your end can come quickly and they are significant.

Computer and network equipment sellers like Dell and Cisco Systems already use digital technology to let business customers handle most of the basic service functions themselves. But this rule applies to the least experienced customer just as much as it does to the sophisticated customer. Holiday Inn's Web-based worldwide reservation system smoothly guides users through the process of locating the hotel nearest their destination, checking availability, taking a virtual tour of the hotel, and completing the reservation. The system even recommends the next closest Holiday Inn if the first choice is full. The process is entirely customer driven, and doesn't require an 800 number or operators at the other end of it.

As these examples suggest, the use of standard-based technology like the Internet can greatly simplify your operation. But how can you convince the customer to do your work? It's easy. For one thing, customers also reduce transaction costs by performing these services themselves. One-time entry of information, as in purchase orders, avoids review, correction, and undetected discrepancies for buyers and sellers, reducing the costs associated with negotiation, policing, and enforcement. Customers who can review product material presale or postsale on an everywhere-everytime basis can also save substantially on search and decision-making costs. The result is the creation of better and more useful data for future uses, including market research, product development, and, not incidentally, richer relationships with your customers.

The Customer Is the Best Customer Service Representative

Consider examples from other industries. In 1995, FedEx built a simple interface into its package-tracking database and made it available to any customer with access to the Internet. The response was overwhelming. Customers had instantaneous access to a detailed history of their package's travels on their own computers. The specificity of the data, which included the exact time packages arrive at interim locations, given in its entirety rather than summarized by an operator, amazed customers and actually enhanced their belief in FedEx's core value proposition of dependable and reliable delivery service. Despite the sometimes erratic performance of the early Web, customers found working on-line easier than calling FedEx, waiting on hold, and then speaking to an operator who was doing little more than reading the contents of a database.

The package-tracking application was launched as an experiment, and a cheap one at that. FedEx bar codes all packages and scans them at every stage of delivery, so the data was already in digital form. By using the World Wide Web and its open standards for text and graphics interfaces, FedEx did not need to invest in expensive software or build a large private network for its customers.

FedEx recognized the killer app potential of its experiment, and went through several quick rewrites of the system, adding features like the digitized signature of the recipient and order entry software that allowed customers to schedule pickups and generate and print airbills (on their own equipment), complete with the bar code. For high-volume users, FedEx created versions of the software that could be downloaded from its site to the customer's computer. With this version, customers perform all these functions off-line and then send the data over the Internet back to FedEx.

For FedEx, the enhancements mean there is only one data entry point, and the customer is responsible for it. For customers, it means never having to type another airbill by hand or run out to a FedEx drop box to pick up any of the various forms. FedEx has already realized savings in the tens of millions of dollars in customer service costs. The customer service representatives, meanwhile, are now free to focus on value-adding interactions with the customer.

Outsourcing the customer service function is also proceeding with breakneck speed in the travel industry, much to the chagrin of travel agents who rely on limited access to rate and package information to justify their commissions from airlines, hotels, and rental car companies. These service providers already compete with agents by offering direct order through 800 numbers, and there has been tension in the industry for years. In 1995 Delta announced it was placing a $50 cap on commissions for most domestic tickets issued by travel agents, and the rest of the airlines soon followed. Travel agents protested, but they no longer had the leverage of exclusive access to customers they once did. Technology has lowered the transaction cost of traveler and carrier finding each other. The commission cut generated $1 billion in revenues during its first year, plenty to be shared between airlines and their customers.

Now, travel reservation and ticketing services in cyberspace are springing up every day. The SABRE Group, one of the leading providers of airline reservation software, launched the Travelocity Web site in 1996, only to find that the immediate response was so great that it had to go through several hardware upgrades just to handle the transaction volume. Using Travelocity, customers have full access to the fare database of all major international airlines. This system's search tools find and rank the best reservation options depending on whether customers prioritize for price, desire for nonstop flight, or maximization of frequent flyer miles. The system eliminates the need for a travel agent for most transactions, reducing customer search costs. In addition, it gives more complete access than calling an individual airline directly, further reducing information costs. On-line self-ticketing already accounts for 4 million tickets a year, largely by the treasured business traveler.

Outsourcing to the customer works as well for manufacturers as it does for service providers. Dell Computers, now the world's leading direct marketer of computer systems, has almost completely shifted its sales and support functions to customer-driven applications and is now selling over $3 million worth of its goods and services *a day* over the Internet. According to the company, its largest corporate, government, and education customers have self-customized Web sites that already know which products customers own when they sign on. The system also provides daily order and manufacturing status. Customers can use the system to configure hardware, choose from a variety of lease/purchase options, and order directly without the need for purchase orders. Customers claim savings in the millions of dollars on technical support and reduced order-processing costs alone.

Those are just the savings on the customer side. For Dell, direct data exchange with customers in cyberspace means speed and reduced costs as well. In the market for desktop computing these advantages are critical. By selling through the Web, Dell doesn't have to wait for dealers to pass the orders on, greatly reducing inventories. Because electronic commerce allows the company to take customer payments directly and immediately, Dell can convert the average order to cash in twenty-four hours. Compare this with the modus operandi of rival Compaq, which continues to operate through dealers. Inventories there are higher, and, more striking, the average order takes 35 days to convert.

The Customer Is the Best Product Developer

Why stop at outsourcing customer service? Why not go further, as some companies have, and outsource the development of future products to customers as well? In many cases customers know best what they need and which features and functions they are willing to pay for. Since they are the end users of these goods and services, they are also experts in how products can and should work. Customers will help you on their own time, when doing so is easy and the rewards—specialized or customized products, faster turnaround times, and even the sense of participation—are tangible.

In the specialized chemicals industry, customer participation in product design is already significant, but the transaction costs for both parties are high. Phone calls, faxes, mailings, and meetings are expensive and erratic. In the filtering of information that goes on between sales and marketing representatives who work with customers, and the product designers who create new products, valuable information is often lost.

To reduce these costs and improve the quality of the information flow, Hüls AG, a leading specialty chemicals manufacturer based in Germany, has begun construction of a virtual design lab. The structure of the lab is simple, using the Web and increasingly cheap high-speed communications to minimize the investment necessary for infrastructure. Hüls plans to use group collaboration tools already available for the Web (such as Livelink), which help distributed project teams organize discussions, share digital work product, and coordinate activities.

In the virtual lab, the worst features of the current process are eliminated. The design process and interaction take place continuously, and communications between customers and developers are direct, avoiding the problem of "helpful" editing. The company believes this environment will support rapid prototyping for new products. In theory, the lower transaction cost environment of the virtual design lab will facilitate a natural movement of the functions involved in design to the participant who has the best information and the most incentive to provide it. That might be Hüls, its subsidiaries, its suppliers, or its customers.

A more extreme example of using digital technology to outsource product development is Firefly, a fast-growing start-up that began life as a project at the MIT Media Lab. MIT professor Pattie Maes had developed some powerful pattern-matching algorithms and decided to let them loose on the Web in the form of a game whose goal was to recommend music that visitors to the site might enjoy. Players ranked their preferences for hundreds of different musical groups and composers, from extreme devotion to "never heard of it." Firefly then told them what other music they might like based on the rankings of other players with similar interests. The more rankings a user gave, the better Firefly did at predicting what he or she would like. The more people who played, the better the predictions got. We had never heard of "The Cowboy Junkies" until Firefly told us that we might like them, and now we're hooked.

Users got to play this fun and possibly eye-opening game for free. Firefly got a product and a company. The popularity of the game quickly created for Firefly a brand name in an exploding market for software "agents," software that learns user preferences and then helps them perform tasks, like shopping, that would otherwise take repetition and time. The company has now licensed its product-selection agents to others, including the Yahoo! search engine and the Barnes & Noble on-line bookstore. The database of music preference profiles, meanwhile, has some of the richest and most credible marketing data on individual musical tastes ever collected.

Customer profiling and targeted marketing are not new, but the ability of an unfunded company to collect high-quality data on a global scale and at almost no cost could only be possible in a world operating under the new forces. Since development of the "product" was outsourced to customers, Firefly could afford to wait and see what kind of revenue models would emerge from its killer app. The company is now pursuing several, including selling ads on its own site, licensing the psychographic data it collects, licensing the agent technology, and selling the items it recommends. One analyst estimated the company's value in 1997 at $100 million.

As all these examples demonstrate, outsourcing to the customer differs significantly from long-standing efforts at cost cutting. In banking, significant cost savings have been realized by shifting customer transactions from branches to telephone and from telephone banking to ATM. But in the shift from ATM to Internet banking, the bank-customer channel is no longer one-way; it is interactive. Internet banking not only reduces costs (replacing the ATM and network with the customer's equipment, for example) but opens up the possibility of expanding, customizing, and cross-selling other goods and services. Given the chance, customers are more than happy to tell you what they want.

2. Cannibalize Your Markets

In traditional planning, managers are justifiably frightened of launching a new good or service that gains market share at the expense of an existing offering. GM's Saturn division has been successful by nearly any measurement, except that it succeeded in large part by siphoning off customers from other GM units. The Saturn story may be more cautionary still, since the company introduced not only a new line of cars that competed with existing brands but also a way of manufacturing, selling, and maintaining cars that may undermine the core assumptions of the entire auto industry. Good for Saturn, but what about for GM?

Executives in our recent survey agreed that technology is redefining the marketplace, upsetting current plans, and allowing unknown, global competitors to spring up overnight, but many seemed paralyzed by a fear that taking action today may cannibalize current operations. Instead, they are trying to hedge their bets with cautious strategies, moving slowly toward cyberspace, and then only with low-risk offerings. A bank executive told us he was using a hybrid telephone/Internet strategy—betting on the Internet in the long term as a major conduit for customer service, betting on the telephone in the short term, and trying to give customers enhanced service using either option.

Hybrid strategies make sense when they are designed for the sake of the customer, but often they are the cover for a hope that a company's past investments can be fully depreciated, a hope that cannot be fulfilled. There is considerable wishful thinking on the part of those, like the CEO of a large retail chain in our survey, who don't think customers are ready to do business with us in cyberspace. Some customers may never want to move. But that group is already smaller than you think.

Cyberspace cannibalism is already rife. Securities broker Charles Schwab offers a 20 percent commission discount and a wide range of software tools to its Internet customers. The *New York Times, San Jose Mercury News,* and others publish their entire daily newspapers on-line, and give away most of the content. The *Wall Street Journal* charges $49 for a full year of unlimited access to its on-line edition, including many services that readers of the printed version don't get for their $150. Even top-drawer management consulting firm Ernst & Young offers a Web-based question and answer service called "Ernie" for $6,000 a year, a price that ought to make its partners blanch.

Are all these companies crazy? Clearly these information-heavy goods and services can be offered at low or no prices because the economics of production and distribution in cyberspace are so dramatically reduced. On-line newspapers don't need to be printed or distributed, on-line brokerage customers don't require the overhead of physical offices, and consultants who can serve clients without getting on airplanes can do so at a greatly reduced price. But what about the current clients and markets? Why don't they immediately shift to the new, lower-priced sales and distribution channel, stranding our current assets, and effectively killing us with our own success?

Part of the answer is that what appears to be cannibalism is no such thing. Ernie is not a replacement for the on-site services of an Ernst & Young consulting team, but a clever way for the firm to leverage its knowledge base of client and industry expertise. It is also a cheap point of entry for new clients who, as they become more successful, can be groomed for the consulting firm's higher-priced services. Many on-line newspapers and Web-based information providers, similarly, are unlikely to be competing with their own print businesses. The *San Jose Mercury News* has few subscribers outside the Bay Area, so offering its news for a greatly reduced price on the Web is largely selling a new product to a new customer base.

Still, some of these examples are genuinely cannibalistic. The *Wall Street Journal* and *New York Times* are national publications, and may limit the sale of their print editions with their impressive on-line offerings. The *Dallas Morning News* made news itself recently by posting a story on its Web site about a supposed confession from Oklahoma City bomber Timothy

McVeigh several hours before its print edition was available, in effect scooping itself. If Charles Schwab and other retail product and service companies are successful in their on-line strategies, they will genuinely threaten their own physical businesses.

There is one obvious reason why these organizations are breaking taboos. If they don't, someone else will. Schwab had to offer lower prices over the Web because start-up competitor E*Trade, which operates solely in cyberspace, was already doing so. Hewlett-Packard recently announced plans to accelerate its promotion of digital cameras in order to grow its $1 billion printer supply business. Doing so puts added pressure on companies like Kodak who are hoping to develop the digital market at their own pace. For news organizations, much of the content comes from wire services anyway, and they know there's nothing that would stop you or anyone else from creating a new business that delivered news solely in electronic form, operating at a drastically lower cost than companies stuck with printing presses and distribution networks.

These cannibals understand that the present value of current channels needs to be balanced against the unrealized power of other information assets they can exploit in cyberspace. Chief among them is brand. New competitors have to build awareness from scratch, but you can jump-start new digital markets with the credibility and goodwill already associated with your organization. Cannibalizing your markets recognizes that the old channels will mature or disappear on their own soon enough, but by taking steps that may hasten that end you can get into the new channel early. The cannibals lead with brand, an information asset that gives them competitive advantage in cyberspace. But only if it is used in time.

Brand must also be used wisely. Cannibalizing markets does not mean cannibalizing the brand itself—that must be kept sacred. Investment bank Hambrecht & Quist may have violated this principle in its launch of a brokerless electronic division whose charter is to sell financial instruments at the same price to consumers as the bank offers to important high-volume institutional customers. According to CEO Donald H. Case III, the company can make up for the cost of smaller transactions with the reduced operating costs of cyberspace and through higher overall volumes. "We'll be the Price Club of electronic financial services," Case said in announcing the service. Institutional buyers might not object too strongly to paying the same price for Hambrecht's services as individuals (assuming they get more individual attention and customized offerings as well), but they might very well object to their prestigious partner repositioning itself as a cheap retailer.

The Stumbling Information Business

The need to cannibalize today's business is particularly acute not just for the newspapers we mentioned earlier but for information providers generally. A closer look at that industry suggests the kind of trauma that is in store for everyone else as the killer apps spread. The news business is already a bits business, and many traditional suppliers of those bits, like wire services, television networks, and newspapers, are resisting the move to digital distribution. Despite its lower cost, digital publishing directly threatens not only existing markets but many time-honored principles of how information providers make and spend their money. Subscription-based newsletters can operate much more cheaply on the Web and reach a much wider audience with minimal additional marketing or operating cost. But once information is released as bits, its natural tendency is to flow, and today's valuable information can be reproduced millions of times with the click of a mouse—legally (the ideas) or illegally (the actual text or broadcast)—by anyone who has access to it. Information providers fear a loss of control over their copyrighted content, and have spent considerable time and money trying to develop digital controls like electronic watermarking. Meanwhile, they are doing little to experiment with the enabling technology itself.

The key for publishers is to recognize that digital media are not simply extensions of current channels any more than TV was a new form of radio. New media require new goods and services, and new attitudes about how to exploit them. The *Wall*

Street Journal's on-line edition signed up 650,000 subscribers during its free trial period. The buzz generated encouraged the paying subscribers after the trial. These subscribers made the experiment profitable in its first year of operation. The free trial demonstrated that the *Journal* on-line was not just a cheaper version of the printed paper but something much more suitable to the capabilities of the Web. The site links stories to more detailed and archival information, hosts discussion forums *between* readers (not just between the paper and the readers, as does today's print op-ed page), and lets subscribers loose on a vast database of up-to-the-minute financial, stock, and company filings, data, and news releases, neatly organized into "briefing books." The site moved from being a cannibalization of the print edition to something that resembles the next generation of product and service the *Journal* will offer, the company's real killer app.

The real lesson of the on-line *Wall Street Journal* is that cannibalization is a healthy symptom of an organization's transformation to a form better able to survive in the new environment. It is a lesson few information providers have learned. Most Web sites associated with TV news services are poorly implemented, and most have failed to win much admiration from their audience in cyberspace. Newspapers haven't done much better. Both are losing out to start-up specialty news providers, most notably CINet, a technology-oriented media company founded in 1992. CINet develops content centrally, then distributes it over a variety of media, including the Web, cable TV, daily E-mail dispatches, and Internet radio. CINet had no market to cannibalize, and its freedom of movement and ingenuity have paid off. Almost half a million subscribers receive the daily bulletins, and the site is one of the most heavily visited on the Web, contacted by up to 3 million users a day.

A Wholesale Cannibal

Wholesalers, as we suggested in Chapter 2, have much to lose from digital technologies' power to reduce transaction costs.

Wholesalers manage the interactions of buyer and seller, reducing the search, information, and negotiating costs that would exist in their absence. Their margin, usually a commission, is based on superior information. As orders-of-magnitude-more information becomes digitized and more easily navigated, markets become transparent, meaning buyers and sellers can find and communicate with each other at far less cost. What, then, is there for a wholesaler to do?

In electronics, wholesaler Marshall Industries understands the threat of the digital killer apps and is trying hard to tame them for its own advantage. Marshall is a $1.2 billion distributor of electronic components and systems for such manufacturers as Siemens, Hewlett-Packard, and Advanced Micro Devices. Before launching itself as an electronic provider, Marshall serviced its 30,000 retailer customers through 37 sales offices located throughout the United States. The company's competitive advantage had been its relationship with major manufacturers and access to a conveniently large inventory.

In 1995, Marshall opened a new channel using the World Wide Web. Technically, the site was a trivial application to develop. Marshall already had a mainframe-based system that was connected over a private network to its sales offices and remotely to the laptops used by its sales force. In effect, the Web site simply offered a new front-end, one based on the Web's multimedia standards. The new interface allowed customers and potential customers from all over the world to search the catalog, place orders, and arrange shipments in a multimedia environment that included audio, video, and foreign language versions.

From the standpoint of Marshall's current business model, the application looks like the corporate equivalent of suicide. Marshall not only lets customers see its price list but provides them with direct links to all of its manufacturing partners, allowing customers to check price and inventory and order directly every item in its catalog. The interface is so easy to use that even current customers might be tempted to switch, cutting off the sales office. In fact, Marshall went further. In regular updates to its site, it has made the Web-based order process even more convenient than its traditional sales channel. All orders are shipped via UPS, for example, and Marshall provides a direct link that allows customers to track their orders using the UPS Web-based system.

What would make a profitable, publicly traded company expend so much energy and enthusiasm on an application that has the potential to wipe out its profit margin? The answer, in part, was recognition by Marshall that even if it didn't open its strategic information to customers, someone else—perhaps the manufacturers—would, and it was better to cannibalize itself than to be eaten. Moreover, this trivial application allowed Marshall to transform itself from a national to a global supplier at almost no cost. The potential loss in one channel is offset by increased volume in another. Marshall receives more than 2,000 inquires a day from 52 countries via its Web site.

Marshall's fearlessness was based on recognition that it had something to offer that went far beyond its role as a manufacturer's representative. Marshall's sales staff has developed significant expertise in product selection, configuration, installation, and postsales support. The company intends to relocate that expertise from the world of atoms to the world of bits; it plans not only to maintain but to expand its market presence by leading with the value it adds to the products it represents. Marshall is well on its way. Its Web site offers on-line seminars, video- and audio-training programs, a twenty-four hour chat room for help, and a collaborative design lab in which customers and Marshall engineers configure custom products. Marshall plans to create extranets with its key accounts, giving manufacturers and customers direct, high-bandwidth and customized access. In effect, Marshall hopes to become the focal point of an electronic marketplace, the organization that can do whatever is necessary not only to bring buyers and sellers together but to ensure quick, successful completion of their transactions.

If the electronic market ultimately replaces your existing business, it's better to be a player in the new channels than an extinct dinosaur remembered for its lack of foresight. Cannibalizing with digital technology can be a low-cost way to find out how soon the change will come, a manageable risk to today's operation. In the end, companies may find that operating as bits-based businesses extends their reach, expands their ability to offer additional goods and services, and even makes them more profitable.

3. Treat Each Customer as a Market Segment of One

A 1997 *Business Week* cover story proclaimed the advent of something it called two-tier marketing—positioning products either to premium buyers (an example would be organic foods) or to value-oriented shoppers (bulk foods). And cable television, we are constantly told, is becoming increasingly specialized as the number of channels increases, a trend known as *narrowcasting*.

The real killer app in marketing is the more dramatic multiplication of product lines that can happen in cyberspace. When goods and services take the form of bits, or even if they just get advertised, wrapped, or shipped with them, the dramatic reductions in transaction costs make it possible for merchants to connect with each customer without the usual set of expensive external and internal intermediaries. Technology makes it possible to create, cheaply and consistently, a customer offering that is unique; not just one time, but every time. Author Stan Davis calls this approach "mass customization," and nowhere is it more viable than in cyberspace.

The Appearance of Personal

Technology-mediated customization is already the rule in bit-intensive information services. Traditional and untraditional news agents are using the Web to unveil increasingly sophisticated tools that let their readers design personal information engines and watch them churn out custom products every day or even every hour. Pointcast has turned the formerly frivolous concept of a "screen saver" into a killer app, delivering content the user wants, from business news to stock reports to sports to gossip, whenever the computer isn't otherwise being used. Excite, another information "push" company, lets its users define their own newspaper front page, including the comics they like, the news that interests them most, a listing of movies playing in their area, and their own personal daily TV schedule, right down to the order of the channels.

Subscribers to the *Wall Street Journal*'s on-line edition can design their own "Personal Journal" and receive dozens of stories from the vast resources of the Dow Jones News Service that otherwise never see print. The system today is simple but effective. Subscribers enter the names of companies and key words of interest to them, and when they sign on each day they are presented with articles that match, organized in an easy-to-use index.

Intuit's Quicken Financial Network goes further, giving users an easy-to-use data entry form to enter their current stock holdings. When subscribers access the site (subscriptions are free, since the site is supported by advertising and is itself an advertisement for Quicken software products), they get an up-to-the-minute report of their portfolio performance, including the current day, overall gains and losses, and a wealth of background information on each of the companies. The reports can be customized by the user or downloaded directly into spreadsheets or Quicken databases. As Intuit expands into other financial services, the company is bringing its customization approach with it. The site now offers tools to create a personal insurance portfolio and a Retirement Planner, which calculates your retirement income before your eyes.

These are simple applications, with considerable room to expand as new media and new technologies, following Moore and Metcalfe, make their way through the Internet incubator (including audio, video, 3D, and real-time chat). Even these early experiments have been exceptionally well received, and have high killer app potential. The *Journal* may be creating a new generation of newspaper, what Professor Negroponte calls "The Daily Me." Quicken is already leveraging its current interface in a move to offer a host of investor, portfolio, and other financial management services.

The power of these applications comes from the fact that customers like the appearance of a personalized product, especially when they have done the personalizing themselves. Modifying the customer-seller equation lowers the transaction costs for customers to get what they actually want (and they may not even know what that is until they begin playing with the free tools). They also become personally vested in the system, often becoming vocal marketers of these services. Think of the religious fervor that has long been the trademark of Apple Computer customers. Imagine tools that create that feeling for your products by offering customers the opportunity to define them or at least choose their packaging.

Treating each customer, if not each transaction, as a unique entity is inexpensive when you use existing (and inexhaustible) digital content and the expanding global computing network. Digital technology creates the miracle of mass customization for a nominal initial cost and then a marginal cost that approaches zero, even on a global scale. There's also a profoundly valuable side effect for you. Customers, in addition to doing their own product design, willingly part with marketing information that most organizations would kill (or even worse, pay) to get their hands on.

The emerging rule in this barter economy is that customers are willing to give away private data in proportion to the direct value they receive in return. Give Travelocity a detailed profile of your travel needs and preferences, and in response you get a selection of itineraries optimized for price and convenience, something beyond the capabilities of your travel agent. Tell Hallmark's Reminder Service the important anniversaries in your life, and they'll E-mail you when it's time to select and send the appropriate greeting. Tell Firefly everything you can about the music you like, and its pattern-matching software tells you what music you're *going* to like. This is a far cry from the warranty cards and direct mail surveys that nearly everyone ignores. When customers see a direct, immediate benefit from cooperating, they're happy to do so, to everyone's advantage.

An Emerging Model in Public Utilities: The Gateway Proposition

Perhaps no industry seems less likely to follow the rule of treating each transaction as a unique event than public utilities like electric, gas, and local telephone providers. These providers rarely seem to recognize, even today, that they have customers in the first place. As long as these markets remain regulated monopolies, where customers have little or no choice, there's really no reason why utilities should care what kind of service they give. Even at rate hike time, the only customers utilities know about are the regulatory agencies, not the "households," "meters," "accounts," or other euphemisms utilities use to refer to their paying subscribers.

But in the United States and Europe, we are seeing just such a revolution in public utilities, one of the chief effects of which is that many are enthusiastically embracing digital technology to customize their offerings to commercial and residential customers. Motivated by rapid deregulation in the United States and the imminent deregulation in Europe as part of its move to a borderless economy, utilities have been scrambling to build bridges and establish meaningful links to their customers as quickly and cheaply as possible. Their hope in doing so is to build brand loyalty before customers get the opportunity to choose their suppliers. Like companies in information businesses, utilities are finding that the fastest way to make that connection is by offering digitally-customized goods and services.

A new model for the utility industry, sometimes referred to as the gateway proposition, is now emerging. In the United States, companies like Utilicorp are already using digital technology to customize offerings around a broad array of services that go beyond basic energy. These include time-of-use or even real-time pricing (based on best available prices in the growing energy commodities markets), remote control of appliances and other equipment, customized billing for corporate customers, and, amazingly, other utility services like telephone, home security, and entertainment. These leading utilities recognize that the electrical connection is just one of many pipelines that serve a home or business.

Ultimately, customers want the option of a single gateway to manage all these pipes—a complete shift that will create opportunity as well as risk for today's providers. Deregulation and an information marketplace make it easy to buy and sell the basic service units, and access to the customer is now seen as the primary objective in an industry with a long history of ignoring that customer's very existence. Companies like Glasgow Electric in Kentucky, which already provides cable television and telephone service as well as electricity, are hoping to be such providers. Just as electricity suppliers are moving into home and commercial services, cable and telephone companies, as well as new asset-free information companies, are moving to control the gateway themselves.

The gateway proposition is a mass-customization strategy based on clever handling of information. As Moore's Law makes it possible to put intelligence into every device (soon down to every lightbulb), Metcalfe's Law spreads out data network standards for communicating with these devices. Homes and businesses will increasingly look like miniature Internets, with the ability to monitor and measure power usage and performance, and adjust devices and rate options to optimize their use of outside services such as power. The goal is nothing less than treating each power usage event, like turning on or off a light switch, as a unique, customized transaction.

Today, enormous quantities of data aren't even captured. But collecting and mining these bits would create significant value for both customer and supplier. Customers would save money and receive precisely the package of energy and related services they want, while utilities could collect information with far more precision than today concerning loads, usage, and other key indicators affecting generation and balancing. Utilities, in real time, could buy and sell excess power on a global market. Consumers and manufacturers could be given or sold performance data on individual appliances that indicate when parts need replacement.

Much of this information, as experiments in the United States and Europe have demonstrated, can be exchanged over the power lines themselves, avoiding today's reliance on the phone network for data communications. It is entirely plausible that the data network inside your home or business will use the existing wiring for infrastructure and follow the open standards of the Internet to communicate both inside and outside.

In our work with German electricity giant PreussenElektra (PE), the progress U.S. utilities have already made with the gateway proposition sounded a wake-up call for management. After our initial presentation, a senior member of its management board confessed that he was "deeply moved" by what he had seen. German power is still highly regulated, but PE knows that significant change is imminent. It also knows that today's complex operating model has left them ill-prepared to treat customers—even its large industrial users like Deutsche Bahn (the German Railway) and Volkswagen—as a market at all, let alone markets of one. Through a network of regional and municipal utilities, PE's power ultimately serves 7 million customers, but today the company has little or no communications with most of them.

The response of the PE management team was swift and definitive. Senior executives began frank discussions with PE's distribution partners, including more than 900 municipal power companies, regarding the development of an "information grid." Teams were dispatched to the United States to visit gateway leaders and to scc others, like Sydkraft in Sweden, that are experimenting with high-speed data transport using the electrical network. PE also began production of its first Web-based customer interface, hoping to begin, before deregulation, a dialogue that will help them expand their information partnership to as many of today's 7 million customers as possible.

As these examples suggest, technology can be employed to create unique goods and services, turning each transaction into an event. The model is already working in news services, travel, retail, and entertainment. It's coming soon, very soon, to everything else, including insurance (design your own policy without an agent), education (where companies like Digital Knowledge

Assets and schools like the University of Phoenix are creating tools for virtual institutions), and even public utilities, as we have just seen.

4. Create Communities of Value

For the last several years, we have taken trips organized and hosted by a company called Backroads. Backroads offers what it calls "active travel." Guests are taken to the most beautiful places in the world and put on bicycles, cross-country skis, or their own two feet and given the opportunity to experience these places from a different vantage point than conventional touring allows. Backroads supplies the tents, cooks the food, and follows discreetly behind in comfortable vans, sending energetic young "hosts" along to ensure everything runs smoothly.

The real value of a Backroads experience, however, is the quality of the other guests. We take such trips because we know that the company attracts like-minded individuals and we know we'll make some new friends by the end of the trip. The Backroads brand stands largely for the quality of its network of customers, who pay, in part, for the opportunity to interact with and be entertained by *each other.*

The success of Backroads, which has grown dramatically to become the leader in active travel, is a Metcalfe magic act. We mention it here to make the point that networks and their distinctly dystrophic economics exist not just in cyberspace. We can hardly think of a more undigital example than Backroads; yet Backroads president Tom Hale has hit on a formula in the physical world that organizations of any size can and should be applying to digital space: creating communities of value by valuing community.

This principle applies with even greater force in cyberspace, since cyberspace is ruled by network economics. Brands rise and fall quickly, communities create their own value as they grow, and low entry and exit costs change many of the rules of competition, disaggregating and reaggregating long-standing industry models. The real power of the new channel is that its architecture allows for high-bandwidth information exchange between merchants and their customers. Even more important, the channel enables powerful communications between the customers *themselves*. This *N*-way interaction, and the value it creates, is what makes electronic commerce a true killer app.

Exploiting the power of communities in cyberspace can be liberating for the company as well as the customer. Mobil Oil built a Web site that attracts visitors interested in Mobil's involvement in Formula One racing. The site cleverly channels its visitors to information about environmental issues important to Mobil. After reading Mobil's side of the story, you're invited to E-mail your elected representatives (which Mobil easily determines based on your zip code) and tell them what you think. If you don't object, Mobil keeps a copy for themselves.

A Web site that appears to be about car racing turns out to be a bold effort to cultivate grassroots political support. Mobil could further enhance the site to allow like-minded visitors to share their views with each other, perhaps in a moderated network discussion hosted by a famous Formula One driver. On-line "cafés" of this sort are already highly evolved on both the World Wide Web (powered by free bulletin board and messaging software from companies like ICQ and The Palace) and on-line services like CompuServe and AOL. The trick will be to direct the tremendous energy being unleashed.

On-Line Services Enable, but Do Not Create, Communities

On-line services and others on the Web have already learned that in building digital community centers, the closer you can get to activities about which the community feels passionate, the greater the potential value you can capture. The computer gaming community has forced its way onto the Internet, building communities even as the technologies they need are being developed. Enthusiasts who have conquered the different levels of the games themselves look to competitive play with others to extend the fun. Game companies are rapidly developing multiuser versions of their programs that can be played by ad hoc collections of players in cyberspace. Meanwhile the gamers are using all the chat and discussion software the Internet has to offer to reduce the transaction costs of finding each other.

Millions of dollars of venture capital are being spent on new businesses that will furnish the environments to connect games and players and serve as independent sources of statistics, rankings, and other information. Winning companies will be those that create the most appealing places to visit, riding the Metcalfe wave in what some analysts project will be a $1 billion market by the year 2002.

The real value in a digital community comes from its participants. Starwave, a start-up company founded by Microsoft cofounder Paul Allen (Disney acquired a significant stake in the company in 1997), built the most successful example of a community of value, the subscription-based ESPN SportsZone service. SportsZone, which leverages the brand value of the all-sports cable TV giant ESPN, is the sports lover's heaven, a virtual locker room attracting millions of visitors a day. In addition to up-to-the-minute sports information, play-by-plays of games in progress, and discussion forums that give Monday morning quarterbacks a high bandwidth channel for self-expression, SportsZone also manages fantasy leagues in which players can draft teams and play against others based on the changing statistics of the real-life players. The more people who sign up for SportsZone, the more additional people who sign up—as pure an example of Metcalfe's Law as we've seen so far.

Even more powerful than the competitive spirit motivating gamers and sports fanatics are matters of the heart. Richard Posner wrote in his provocative economic analysis of human relations, *Sex and Reason,* that modern urban life has dramatically increased the transaction costs for finding suitable spouses, friends, and sexual partners. Walk into any singles bar and you'll see why. The darkness, noise, and altered mental state of the patrons increase, rather than reduce, search and information costs.

Cyberspace provides an alternative. While imperfect, it is still an enormous improvement. Though consultants John Hagel and Arthur Armstrong write extensively about on-line services like America Online (AOL) in *Net Gain,* their study of virtual communities, they overlook its most valuable feature: the chat rooms, bulletin boards, and "instant message" dialogues. These features enable real-time communication between members of a fast-growing subscriber base, creating the environment for communities of friends and lovers to form with dramatically reduced transaction costs. (It's true that AOL *advertises* itself largely on the basis of its content, but most of that is available in better form for free on the World Wide Web. Few AOL subscribers we know go anywhere near these areas.)

AOL builds these communities of value simply by attracting as many users as possible. Members are given the tools they need to find and communicate with each other in what AOL calls its "People Connection" service. There, members create their own "rooms" based on personal interests, including location, sexual preference, or even frivolous topics. Other AOL members can access the room and participate in private or room-wide discussions, or create private rooms just for their friends. The system maintains "Buddy Lists" that tell members when their friends sign on and off and where they are, a feature AOL recently extended to users of the entire Internet.

AOL provides a safe context in which users meet, the technology to interact, and, most of all, the membership itself. The communities form, operate, and disband entirely on their own. The popularity of this service—there are hundreds of rooms open all day and night—prefigures dramatic changes even in industries only peripherally involved in human relations (like clothing, entertainment, and alcoholic beverages) as well as patterns in future demographics (such as location).

Compare "People Connection" with Digital City, a service AOL runs in over 20 cities together with local information providers like newspapers, available both within AOL and on the Web. Digital City is an explicit attempt to build digital community centers for urban populations, giving its users one-stop shopping for information about neighborhoods, restaurants, housing, events, and classified ads.

Digital City fails, however, to follow the very rule that has made AOL successful. Content is provided by publishers of newspapers like the *Chicago Tribune,* and these partners bring an information "broadcast" approach to a medium where broadcast is not only unnecessary but an insult. Digital City Chicago, for example, provides restaurant and movie reviews written by the *Tribune*'s staff critics as well as information about housing and neighborhoods provided exclusively by sellers and landlords. There is, remarkably, no way for users to post their own reviews or otherwise share their expertise about the community, and there is no mechanism for using Digital City to find and exchange information with anyone other than these "official" sources. The design reflects a profound misunderstanding by the media companies about the power of the new media, a further example of the tremendous confusion information businesses are experiencing at the hands of the killer apps.

Communities and Brands

The value of AOL is the value of the network, not the content. The monthly charge is a fee for access to that network. Keeping that fee low brings in more members, increasing the value of the product, which AOL can leverage by selling other goods, services, or advertising. Recognizing this balance, AOL switched from hourly billing to a monthly fee for unlimited access, only to discover that it had vastly underestimated the appeal of its own product. Users spent more time on-line, which encouraged other users to want to do the same, and the company's network infrastructure (the private one, not the Internet, as many newspapers reported) was overwhelmed—a Metcalfe misjudgment. Members suddenly found themselves waiting an hour or more just to get connected.

The ensuing rage of customers spread to other communities, including a forum created by the *New York Times* at its Web site, and even caught the attention of state attorneys-general, most of whom probably didn't even know what an on-line service was. A similar revolt occurred later when AOL considered leasing the phone numbers of its members to merchants, despite having promised not to do so. CEO Steve Case received so much E-mail that within twenty-four hours he changed course and announced that the phone lists would not be released after all.

AOL is not a stupid or an evil company. As a pioneer in the development of communities of value, it is likely to continue bumping into the Law of Disruption when it makes missteps like these. (Wall Street seems to understand this—during the period when these disasters occurred, AOL's stock climbed from $22 to $70 a share.) The rest of us will learn these lessons, too. As digital technology pursues its Metcalfe invasion of the home and the global computing network becomes a part of day-to-day life, the transaction costs of community organizing are plummeting. For customers, the power to interact is also the power to band together and express collective will on businesses of all kinds, something most companies rarely needed to worry about in the predigital past. In AOL's case, customers were actually provided with the tools that were used to put pressure on the company.

The more general point is that communities of value play a powerful role in developing and managing brand. Brands, as we've said, serve as the shorthand for a company's qualities. On the one hand, digital technology makes it possible to communicate brand to a growing number of constituencies (not only customers but suppliers, shareholders, regulators, and other business partners) at a rapidly decreasing cost. The same technology creates a corresponding risk that deviations from those qualities can also be communicated, quickly and effectively, by customers and competitors (consider the "Untied Airlines" site, which is a rich information source on examples of poor service from United). Consumers long shielded from negative "advertising" may overvalue its importance when it suddenly starts to flow, as airlines learn whenever there is an accident. Good news travels fast, but bad news travels even faster. As Mark Twain once said, "A lie travels halfway around the world while the truth is still putting its shoes on."

Customers who aren't given an official forum in which to express their feelings about branded goods and services may take advantage of Moore's Law and Metcalfe's Law to create their own, with unexpected consequences. Executives at a well-known maker of an international brand of beer asked recently whether it was time to establish a presence in cyberspace. We did a simple search of the Web and discovered that there were already thousands of homepages carrying information about their product, most of them from enthusiastic consumers. Many of them identified themselves as the product's "official" home-page, and several were offering free audio and video clips from the company's advertising—even screen savers based on the company's commercials.

Such displays of product devotion are the dream of every marketer and the point of advertising and promotions in the first place. For our client, however, their ignorance of an intense unofficial ad campaign already taking place on the Internet had the makings of a nightmare. Even if the company wanted to enforce its legal rights to control the use of its brand and intellectual property (the screen savers unquestionably violated copyrights), doing so had become impossible. There were too many customers to stop. Imagine, as well, the response to a lawsuit against a customer who was proclaiming to the world that your product was a defining element of his life. The better solution would have been to start by asking not *whether* they should have presence but how best to channel it. And to have asked the question before customers took matters into their own hands.

Brand management in cyberspace requires real engagement with customers. You need to ensure that their good experiences become bits that enhance the value of your information assets; you also need to provide a moderated forum to air their bad experiences. Even complaints can become valuable bits. Answering questions or complaints quickly can cement a lifelong relationship with a customer, but responding slowly, inappropriately, or not at all can be extremely damaging to the organization's brands. Worse, it may encourage or even empower customers to find other avenues. Experience so far suggests that this feature of the new business environment is poorly understood. Many organizations confess to being overwhelmed by the level and volume of communication they receive via E-mail, much of which they invite on their homepages.

Business-to-Business Communities

You don't have to sell sports or sex to build valuable communities. Though the stories of SportsZone and AOL are dramatic, most organizations start their community-building activities around more traditional activities, like relationships between buyers and suppliers. These relationships, after all, are limited by transaction costs that make it difficult for business partners to find each other and to share information. Organizations in many industries are experimenting with digital technology to increase the size and scale of their business-to-business networks, finding along the way that doing so not only reduces costs but creates new value.

One of our clients, for example, is a large developer and manager of residential real estate that owns several hundred thousand units of housing. To help it coordinate the assignment of repair work to various craftsmen, the company built a computer system, which it operated over a proprietary data network, that made the repair data electronically available to approved contractors. The text-only system allowed the company to send work orders directly to craftsmen without the need for paperwork, saving time and money.

The company now wants to take advantage of the decreasing cost and improved network possibilities of using the Internet. Compared with their private network, the Internet is open and easily scalable, and using it would allow them to connect to many more service providers at a lower operating cost. The Internet already offers a richer set of interface-building tools than the old system, and promises, through its open standards, the future possibility of videoconferencing and direct access to the devices, such as major appliances, in the rented homes.

The company is building an Internet-based network to replace the private system and in the process has completely changed its understanding of what such an application can do. They now see that their business-to-business connections can be easily changed and expanded, allowing them to add in and switch out not only contractors but also suppliers of building materials, the tenants themselves, and other stakeholders, including banks, local governments, and construction companies.

The new network will allow our client to provide many new and enhanced services. In addition to giving suppliers, craftsmen, the company, and its tenants a common area in which to transact business, the company can consolidate materials orders from the craftsmen, obtain discounts from suppliers, and provide short-term financing for materials. In exchange for guaranteeing volume for the craftsmen, the company can obtain better rates and improve overall quality. Once the company has used the network to remake itself into a service provider, it might even scale up further by offering its expertise to other property management companies.

Summary

The new economics of cyberspace dramatically alter the ways in which organizations interact with customers, suppliers, and markets, presenting the potential for a wide range of killer apps to be created and used to manage these new relationships. We have presented four design principles for shaping this new environment. Many of them might seem counterintuitive or worse. In the context of the new forces, however, each of these rules makes good business sense. In cyberspace, customers want to do our work for us, cannibalizing markets is necessary to our survival, customizing every product for every customer is possible and inexpensive, and enhancing communities rather than markets will create the best opportunities to extract new margin.

These strategies have already been tested in a variety of industries, often with great success. Companies like FedEx, Firefly, AOL, and even public utilities are creating new competitive landscapes using today's most interesting digital technologies.

5

building new connections

What unity do we find in the various aspects of bad faith? It is a certain art of forming contradictory concepts which unite in themselves both an idea and the negation of that idea.
—Jean Paul Sartre

Life which is one continuous struggle with other men is hardly worth living.
—Frederick Winslow Taylor

THE FOUR DESIGN principles covered in this chapter concern the construction of interfaces between you and your business partners, including customers, suppliers, and even competitors:

5. Replace rude interfaces with learning interfaces.

6. Ensure continuity for the customer, not yourself.

7. Give away as much information as you can.

8. Structure every transaction as a joint venture.

These principles flow logically from the principles presented in Chapter 4, which dealt with building killer apps to interact with the inhabitants of cyberspace in bold new ways. The new relationships require new, dramatically different connections that will bind you to business partners in ways that are as rich as the physical ties that hold your organization together today. The difference is that tomorrow's interfaces will be virtual, adherents rather than victims of the Law of Disruption. Many organizations already find that they are having better information exchanges with outsiders than with insiders, a symptom of the widening gap in technology adoption between firms and the market.

As the Law of Diminishing Firms predicts, moreover, the distinction between what is inside and what is outside is constantly shifting. The new interfaces you create consequently need to be rich in content and function (including entertainment value). They must be fluid, transparent, and easily modified or even rebuilt. Building them with the Internet's open standards and on its nonproprietary global computing networks is not only cost-effective but leads to a more robust result than do the hardware and software you may be accustomed to using. Thanks to the network properties of Metcalfe's Law, speedy enhancement and a ruthless marketplace for superior innovations have kept the pace of improvement on the Net breathtaking.

What might also surprise you is the way you use these interfaces to structure the new transactions. The design principles for building new connections contradict a lot of conventional wisdom. We demonstrate how companies develop killer apps by replacing human interfaces with computer systems and yet still achieve "customer intimacy." This is actually easy to do, in part because the industrial time-and-motion approach to process management has already taken the life out of most customer interactions. What organizations think of as intimate is often just the opposite. Digital technology (thanks to Moore) and a growing body of multimedia interface tools give you the power to build, and build cheaply, superior channels of communication with all your business partners. Replacing human contacts with digital interfaces not only lowers transaction costs but accelerates the process of capturing new information in bits, allowing you to multiply its value.

With a new digital pipeline in place, organizations decide how much of their proprietary data to keep "behind the firewall," that is, away from the other members of its community of value. The new forces—deregulation, digitization, and globalization—require a major shift in attitude. In the old world, proprietary information was a key weapon in achieving leverage over business partners. Now much of what you consider proprietary, like designs, customer lists, and market intelligence, is readily available elsewhere in reusable digital form. In any case, your proprietary data has a greatly reduced time value. In contrast, granting wide access to proprietary data to your business partners, including competitors, invokes Metcalfe's Law, generating new value as the information spreads. In our experience, organizations often overvalue secrecy and underestimate the value of sharing data instead. Those who take proprietary information often return it in more valuable condition.

Other assumptions about the behavior of markets and industries will also be undermined as you begin to translate new environmental conditions into new interfaces that exploit them. Senior executives, for example, often confuse their own difficulties (technical and cultural) in transitioning to cyberspace with those of their business partners. Their suppliers aren't ready to talk about more dynamic and flexible partnerships, they tell us, unsure really of who those suppliers are, let alone how the suppliers' world is changing. They believe customers don't have computers, aren't hooked up to the Internet, or aren't ready to buy and sell over the World Wide Web, but they haven't bothered to ask the customers if this is so.

The truth is that consumers understand and embrace the trend toward decentralized buying and selling through technology interfaces much more readily than sellers do (think of catalogs, 800 numbers, and television shopping). Consumers are only waiting for critical mass. The smart thing might even be to pay for their Internet access, since the reduced transaction costs of, say, electronic billing, might alone justify the investment in a few months.

5. Replace Rude Interfaces with Learning Interfaces

The human touch isn't quite as warm as it used to be. Even in the retail industry, where direct customer contact is constant, companies—like Nordstrom's, FedEx, or the Four Seasons hotels—that provide consistently good service are the awe-inspiring exception, not the rule. In a *New York Times* story about the decline of customer service, a customer of Filene's department store in Boston reported that after an exceptionally unfriendly transaction, she told the clerk, "A thank you would be nice." To which the clerk responded, "It's written on the receipt."

Well, why not be rude? No organization is immune to a mass revolt (or even a credible threat) by all of its customers, but imagine the transaction costs of a single customer informing all the others of any bad experience. Worse still, think of how hard it is even in local markets for consumers to band together to punish poor service or overpriced goods. Even in long-distance phone service, where rate setting has been turned over to a highly competitive market for more than ten years, overall industry profitability is still astronomical. In theory, consumers have the power to force an industry to the point of bare profitability overnight. But that's only theory. In practice, collective action problems are everywhere, and the costs for customers of organizing and sharing information as a group have been prohibitively high.

Now, thanks to digital technology, those costs are coming down, forcing organizations to reevaluate which if any of their customer contacts are really helping the cause. Superior customer service, or what consultants Michael Treacy and Fred Wiersema call "customer intimacy" in *The Discipline of Market Leaders,* is part of the mission statement of every organization we know. For most, it's a mission impossible. A senior vice president at AT&T once told us with a straight face that his company was "intimate" with 80 million customers a day.

It Can Only Get Better

Stop for a moment and think about the five most recent direct contacts you've had *as a consumer* with the checker at the grocery store, an airline reservation agent, the customer service department of your credit card company, or even a directory-assistance operator. Did you receive superior customer service? Did you receive any service at all? Did you think to yourself that you'd just as well take your business elsewhere if only you weren't convinced it would be just as bad? And, even if you did receive superior service, was there any indication that the company collected the information you gave it, so that it could better serve you next time? Did the company give *you* the opportunity to structure the transaction the way you wanted?

Every direct contact with the customer is an opportunity to improve the relationship and to learn more about the customer's needs. But most customer contacts offer little or no opportunity to do either. One of the reasons customers have responded so well and adapted so easily to FedEx's on-line package tracking application (see Chapter 4) is that the human operator who had managed the old system wasn't really acting like a human being in the first place. All he or she did was type the user's input and read back the response from a computer screen. Human beings, it turns out, make very poor computer peripherals.

We know one commercial bank that prides itself on its close relationships with its customers in small businesses, a relationship the bank refers to in its advertising as a partnership. The bank adopted a policy guaranteeing that every customer phone call would be answered by a human being rather than an automated system. A complex rollover mechanism ensures that even if an account executive is unavailable, the call is routed to an assistant. The theory is that in the absence of the executive, the assistant can provide a "human touch" that voice mail cannot.

In practice, the assistants do little more than take messages and, more often than not (usually at the customer's insistence), transfer the call to voice mail anyway. Worse, after 5 P.M., the assistants have gone home and there is no way to get into the bank's voice mail system. When there are no human beings to provide the "human touch," the phone just rings off the hook.

An alternative solution, one that recognizes the power of digital technology, would have been to improve the disliked voice mail interface. Wildfire, a voice-driven "electronic telephone assistant," has done just that. Wildfire does many remarkable things, including screening, routing, and announcing your calls; it "whispers" in your ear when new calls are trying to get through so you can decide whether or not to take them, and it maintains a virtual phone book of your most frequently dialed numbers. Wildfire improves the likelihood that the call will get to you in the first place, solving the real problem the bank had identified.

So even though technology-based interfaces (a voice mail system instead of an operator, an ATM machine instead of a bank teller, a kiosk instead of an information desk) can be cold and inflexible, at least they're predictable. They are already improving many transactions in which the operator merely served as a computer interface device, including most banking, billing, order entry, and order status applications. Technology interfaces are almost never rude. Some even speak more than one language. And soon they will be able to handle voice as well as text and graphics.

Digital interfaces are making especially good progress in industries with long histories of unpleasant customer interactions (retail, insurance, and government, to name three), where they provide both lower cost and higher quality. For a demonstration, visit a Web-based telephone directory like Four11 or the FedWorld site for tax forms and taxpayer information. New York City has deployed experimental kiosks, which deliver a range of the services provided by City Hall throughout Manhattan. One user of the kiosks described the interface as being "like a New York City worker who works 24 hours a day, and it's more friendly."

But digital technology can do better than offering service that is merely not impolite. As many recent examples demonstrate, it is already possible to build superior customer interfaces that mediate human interaction, providing quick and efficient automated service at a level defined by the customer. Like video games, on which they are modeled, these interfaces adapt automatically to users' levels of skill, advancing them through the system's functions as they are ready and calling on a human being when the situation requires one. Equally important, these interfaces record their interactions, providing a rich store of data. We call such systems "learning interfaces," a phrase coined by computer scientist Alan Kay.

Several start-up companies are experimenting with learning interfaces today, often with very positive consumer response. GetSmart is a service that currently helps users find the best-fitting credit card, mortgage provider, or mutual fund. Consumers are guided through the process of selecting and ranking criteria they may not have even realized were important, and the system responds with follow-up questions and, ultimately, the opportunity to apply for the best-fitting solution. GetSmart's learning interface lowers the transaction cost of buyers and suppliers finding each other. An independent company, its revenue comes from referral fees paid by the suppliers once the transaction is complete.

Seattle-based Netbot, Inc., has gone even further with its Jango product, which was acquired in October 1997 by the Excite network. Jango is your personal shopping agent for a fast-growing variety of products being sold in cyberspace. You describe what you're looking for and rank your selection criteria. Jango scours the Web for you, returning with a detailed list of offering vendors. The list highlights what can be a remarkable range of prices for even standard products like laptop computers or music CDs. The product is all interface; over time, it will be able to learn and adapt to your preferences, further reducing the transaction costs of electronic commerce.

Eliminating Customer Sacrifice

One of the most valuable features of a learning interface is that it gives the merchant an understanding of what consultant Joe

Pine has termed "customer sacrifice." Customer sacrifice is the difference between what a customer settled for and what the customer would have wanted in the best of all possible worlds. Consider home grocery delivery pioneer Peapod. Peapod's Web-based service provides customers a high-quality selection and ordering function (even for items such as produce typically judged by appearance and smell). Subscribers access the system over the Web and submit orders to Peapod electronically. For a fee, Peapod picks the inventory at one of its partners' stores and delivers it directly to the customer. Peapod is now doing significant business, with 45,000 subscribers by mid-1997.

With its direct access to customer preferences, Peapod is teaching its grocery store chain partners more than they bargained for about customer sacrifice. Before Peapod, according to a senior executive at one large chain, the company believed that its ability to meet the customer's needs was extraordinary, given customer satisfaction ratings that were typically 96 percent. But an analysis of Peapod's records demonstrated otherwise. Since customers could identify their first and second choices, the data demonstrated precisely when the store did not have the merchandise the customer wanted. The reality was that Peapod shoppers got what they wanted only 70 percent of the time. "That information startled the hell out of everybody," he told us. It also provided the data needed to fix the problem.

Replacing human interfaces is by no means a downsizing strategy. Customer contact personnel freed from these mechanical interactions can focus instead on meaningful customer exchanges, including new customer development and working with existing customers to identify additional services the company could provide. More importantly, learning interfaces transform the customer interaction into two-way conversations. The immediate benefit of these conversations to the seller is that they know instantly when they are not serving the customer's needs. Over the longer term, the learning interface becomes the primary mechanism for creating the communities of value we described in Chapter 4. Enhancing the interface to let customers talk to each other as well as to you changes the dialogue from two-way to *N*-way. That, at least, is the beginning of community.

6. Ensure Continuity for the Customer, Not Yourself

Hoping to stall the painful move from the world of atoms to the world of bits, many of our clients begin by hiding behind their customers. The mass market isn't ready for this, they say. People are afraid of computers. The Internet is scary. Scary for whom? There's little doubt that digital technology and the killer apps they enable are making life difficult for most everyone in business. Old ways of doing business disintegrate overnight, reducing the time to respond from years to days. For customers many of the changes are beneficial. More to the point, they are entirely consistent with developments in commercial life consumers have been enjoying for years. The Law of Disruption is what you have to worry about. Managing continuity for customers and other business partners means doing what you can to protect them from the fallout.

Andy Lippman, director of the MIT Media Lab's Digital Life program, which studies the social dimension of computing, made this point eloquently during a recent consulting project. The client, a group of related trading and transportation companies, was concerned that its customers and suppliers would be uncomfortable switching to electronic interfaces. But why worry about that? Lippman asked. They deal with electronic interfaces all day—the telephone, the television, ATMs, grocery scanners, car dashboards, even automated bus transfers. Customers don't know, or don't care, that technology has replaced familiar ways of doing things when the interface is designed to continue the old metaphors. Digital gauges on dashboards still "look" like gauges. Electronic bingo cards, in another example, are designed to simulate blotting out called numbers.

Electronic commerce, in essence, combines the unhurried convenience of catalog shopping with the superior interface of TV shopping, innovative developments that customers adapted to almost from inception. (Revenue from TV shopping will reach $60 billion in the United States by the year 2000 at its present rate of growth.) Table 5.1 compares the different perceptions of electronic commerce held by customers and merchants. The table highlights how the migration to electronic commerce disrupts the activities of merchants in ways that are perceived by consumers as incremental improvements to interfaces they already know.

For customers electronic commerce is like an interactive catalog, supplemented with audio, video, and (eventually) real-time interaction with other shoppers. The merchant, on the other hand, must deal with the fact that electronic commerce erases much of the value of physical stores, which must be transformed into showrooms, demo centers, or staging areas for direct home delivery. As customers grow to expect customized goods not just for information products but for manufactured goods— blue jeans, cars, and home computers, for example—manufacturers will need to find ways of using technology to improve production and delivery systems by several orders of magnitude, adding memory, perhaps, that stores the customer's specifications.

TABLE 5.1

Electronic Commerce—Continuous to Consumers and Disruptive to Merchants

	Consumer	*Merchant*
Location	The best of catalog and TV shopping	Electronic access beats placement; stores become showrooms and warehouses
Marketplace	An expanded horizon	The market is the world
Intelligence	The store now knows consumer	The consumer is the database
Purchasers	Junk mail gets smart	Agents do the buying
Brand, Branding	Shopping is a social experience	Word of mouth grows in importance
Goods	One size fits consumer	Smart goods are arriving; trucks become manufacturers
Payment	Value becomes evident; instant payment equals instant refund; consumer buys what he or she wants	Micropayment creates microtransactions

Final assembly will have to be outsourced to the delivery system itself, turning trucks into miniature manufacturing plants.

Several electronic commerce start-up companies are building businesses that do nothing but minimize disruption for customers and merchants. Cybercash, for example, was launched to solve the difficult problem of handling electronic payments cheaply, safely, and without having to utilize relatively high-cost credit card systems that do not respond well to large volumes of low-price transactions.

Cybercash initially offered a simple third-party verification service to belay exaggerated fears of credit card fraud by customers who were being told by credit card companies that the Web was not a safe place to reveal their account numbers. (It is, in fact, as safe as doing so over the telephone or in stores with electronic card readers.) Cybercash, and rivals DigiCash and Mondex, have since launched experiments in providing technology that acts like cash ("E-cash"). E-cash is stored on intelligent credit cards that can be plugged into computers or given to participating merchants. Mondex has already coordinated merchant and customer immersion pilots in England and Canada and on New York City's Upper West Side.

Customers will grow comfortable with E-cash initially because it will simulate the familiar experience of using paper bills and coins. Eventually they will learn that electronic money has advantages over cash, which will lead to new uses. E-cash can be programmed (so that, for instance, parents can limit what their children buy with it), it can be switched from one currency to another without incurring high transaction fees, and it can generate mountains of useful data as it is used to help fine-tune buying decisions and products. The key will be to bring the customers along as quickly and as smoothly as possible, not as slowly as is convenient or most profitable for the developers. As one Mondex user put it, "Convenience is addictive."

WebTV's CEO, Steve Perlman, ran an end-run around computer manufacturers that were scampering to build cheap Internet access devices by playing to the customer's preference for the familiar. Perlman recognized that many consumers don't want a computer at all, only access to the Internet for features like the Web and E-mail. Since every home in the United States already has television, which owners are entirely comfortable operating, Perlman's killer app is to use technology to extend the TV rather than to introduce a new, unfamiliar device. Instead of forcing consumers to accept the computer makers' mind-set, Perlman adopted the consumer's perspective, and transformed televisions into simple Web access devices by connecting them to a phone line, remote control, and optional keyboard, coupled with a subscription-based access service oriented toward nontechnical (and happily so) users.

Don't Project Your Hang-Ups into Cyberspace

In launching digital goods and services, too many organizations do just the opposite of what WebTV did. They try to minimize their own disruption at the cost of adding confusion for the customer. When United Airlines announced its electronic ticketing feature in 1996, the launch included a ridiculous ad that suggested E-tickets solved a pressing problem for travelers: the risk of losing their tickets. "Even this guy couldn't lose our latest airline ticket," the ad said, showing a businessman with papers coming out of every corner of his briefcase.

But who really worries about losing their airline ticket? The real advantage of the E-ticket was enjoyed by United, which could bypass the ticketing charge from the organization that assigns unique numbers to physical tickets. The approach that would have been understandable to passengers would have simply been to offer sharing some of this cost savings with early adopters, like the members of their frequent flyer program, until the new system became familiar enough to pitch to occasional travelers as a true convenience.

Electronic tickets actually created more hassle for travelers. Gate personnel were poorly trained to handle them, and airport security personnel still don't understand, a year later, why passengers are unable to show them a ticket, as is required to get access to the gate. Without a paper ticket, it's difficult to switch at the last minute to another airline if United's flight is delayed or canceled. Instead, United wished away these problems, and the result is that passengers are still confused by the new "service."

Failures to manage customer continuity are easy to find on the Web. Motorola, a leading manufacturer of other people's killer apps, had until recently a nearly impenetrable Web site that was organized not around the different ways customers were likely to visit but around its own internal structure. To find information on a good or service, you first had to determine which of several similarly named business units made it. We went in search of information about the sports paging device that was the subject of the lawsuit between Motorola and the National Basketball Association mentioned in Chapter 2, but never found it, getting lost in a maze of data about satellite systems and wireless protocol standards.

It is difficult, perhaps, for large bureaucratic organizations like Motorola to break down internal barriers and share information with each other, but it is a particularly bad idea to reveal these institutional infirmities to customers and frustrate their efforts to do business with you in the process. Compare to Motorola the genuinely engaging site of Toyota. This site was developed not internally but by Saatchi & Saatchi, Toyota's advertising agency. Saatchi & Saatchi clearly understood the value of customer-centered interface design. The Toyota site does not bore you or confuse you by telling you anything about how Toyota sees itself but tries instead to create for you the experience of being a Toyota owner. Using attractive graphics, video clips, and text that projects an engaging, edgy attitude, the Toyota site combines the best elements of advertising, test drives, and slick car brochures. Together they tell the user a story about what it is like to be a Toyota driver. The secret was developing the interface for the customer, not the company.

Evolving Interfaces Smooth the Transition

Starting with the customer's viewpoint is only part of the solution. Your interface must also bring the customer along as he or she is most comfortable from the old world to the new. The interface is the tool for doing so. This is the strategy being followed by the best of the banking and retail sites on the Web today. Security First Network Bank, the Internet-only bank, initially presented itself with a three-dimensional model of a bank branch office. Click on the information desk and learn about the bank. Click on a teller and you were transferred to transaction processing. Click on the security guard and you learned how the bank's assets are insured by the U.S. government. As customers became more familiar with the added capability of the new media, Security First's site evolved along with them. The site now minimizes the branch office picture and instead customizes the interface dynamically based on the customer's previous activities and identified preferences. In late 1997, the company evolved even further and decided to sell the bank itself and concentrate on software and services to help other banks make the move to cyberspace.

Our trading and transport client decided, based on these examples, to organize its electronic offering around the concept of the customer's home, since most of its goods and services are aimed, one way or another, at homeowners. The breakdown of activities between the different divisions will be hidden from the users, who will see an interface that walks them through the familiar activities of home improvement. This client will eventually expand its offerings and bring in related functions, like security services, home buying and selling, and management of the various systems inside the home. Ultimately the interface will become a part of the house. Our client will need to make massive changes to achieve these objectives. But its customers won't.

7. Give Away as Much Information as You Can

In the early 1980s, health care manufacturer Baxter Travenol enjoyed considerable competitive advantage over competitors by letting customers submit orders directly to Baxter's computer system. To do this, the company placed terminals in the order departments of hospitals, making it easy for purchasing personnel to buy from Baxter. The terminals gave hospitals access only to Baxter's catalog, but ordering electronically was easier than filling out paperwork, and once used to the Baxter system, the hospital was loath to learn a new one or to accept the terminal of a competitor.

Baxter's system was a closed network, the user equivalent of the strategy in full force in the computer industry in the early 1980s. IBM locked in its customers by selling them equipment that ran only IBM systems software, which in turn supported applications that were written only for the IBM system. Similarly, its data communications network, SNA, ran only on and between IBM processors. Most of the other computer companies at the time pursued a similar strategy. Once locked in to a closed standard, customers were unwilling to incur what economists call switching costs, giving suppliers a captive market.

The age of closed systems is over, and companies like IBM, DEC, and several European computer manufacturers that built their empires on them have either disappeared or made the painful switch to open architectures and open systems. The new world is fueled by open systems, and the few holdouts in both systems and application software will inevitably give up. In designing killer apps, the rule for the interface is always to make it as open as possible and to give away information rather than hoard it.

The primary forces behind this transformation are once again Moore's Law and Metcalfe's Law. Moore's Law makes it possible to spread new applications across global computing networks cheaply and efficiently, dramatically lowering switching costs. Metcalfe's Law, meanwhile, extends the number of people who can innovate with the system and consequently who can increase its value.

Baxter's system only let customers send orders. It did not give them access to other interesting bits Baxter might have had, closing off the potential for customers to create new transactions themselves. IBM, similarly, was determined to use SNA as insurance for its corporate strategy of keeping computing hierarchical, reliant at the top on the mainframe computers from which IBM made its highest profits. This meant that SNA development had to be kept strictly internal, and all that was ever revealed to customers was the minimum they needed to use it.

SNA was soundly defeated by the Internet's decentralized communications protocols, which had no corporate backing but were instead being developed by a research lab made up of the entire world. Because everyone has access to the standards and can propose changes to them, new directions and new uses are possible. The Internet evolved organically into a nonhierarchical network, where every device—even cheap ones—can participate fully. This architecture, because of its unlimited scalability, has proven critical for unleashing killer apps, and the force of its added value overcame one of the greatest marketing organizations in history.

The Decline of Switching Costs

Imagine a start-up health care supplier of today competing with the Baxter Travenol of the early 1980s. Where Baxter operates and maintains its own computer network, including the processors, communications links, and individual terminals, the start-up will piggyback its order entry system off the Internet, which any customer can easily access with a range of devices. The modern competitor can also build its software out of inexpensive, powerful components like multimedia browsers and the ever-expanding extensions and plug-ins that feed the World Wide Web.

What's more, the new competitor can take advantage of the very openness of the Web to proffer links not only to customers but to distribution partners (a FedEx or a UPS) and to product manufacturers themselves (including Baxter). As a result, the start-up will offer a wider selection of products, better prices, and more flexible delivery options, and it could operate at substantially lower cost than the closed Baxter environment. Its margin is derived from the system's openness, in other words, not from the captive market. This is essentially the business model that wholesaler Marshall Industries has adopted in the electronics components business (see Chapter 4). It could and is being replicated in many other markets.

The destruction of captive markets signals the decline of switching costs for customers. Switching costs are not unheard of in the open environment, but they are of a very different—and fragile—nature. Switching costs are easier to overcome, as a general rule, the less they depend on locking customers into inflexible alternatives. A Gillette razor has high switching costs because changing your source of blades requires you to change the hardware. Software, including IBM's SNA, is easier to replace.

When the interface is built on open standards, switching costs can be established, if at all, only for the actual information users provide to the system. Users of Intuit's financial software, for example, or of Charles Schwab's e.Schwab, invest considerable time entering personal financial and investment data into proprietary databases supported by these programs. This investment creates the potential for an information switching cost. Even if the customer eventually finds another piece of software preferable, say Microsoft Money or E*Trade, switching would require reentry of the customer's information and time to learn the differences between the old system interface and the new one.

Unlike hardware and even software, however, information switching is less disruptive and easier to avoid. Building a bridge from your competitor's interface to yours would be next to impossible at the hardware level. Building a razor that takes Gillette blades would almost surely violate a patent (in effect a regulated switching cost). Courts have gradually ruled, in contrast, that information formats and interface "look-and-feels" are not entitled to such extreme protection, limiting the ability of interface developers to lock users in. A competitor today can easily build a conversion program to transfer your data to its format, as many software products in generic categories like word processing, spreadsheets, and graphics have already done. And the pressure is building, not easing, for Web-based interfaces to support common standards as a starting point for both data and look-and-feel.

Dying with Their Boots On

Some organizations remain committed to closed interactions with customers and appear ready to go down fighting rather than make the painful but potentially liberating switch to growing global networks and standards. In the market for legal information services, two dominant competitors, LEXIS/NEXIS and West, offer their information services to lawyers exclusively through private networks and proprietary software. Both began experimenting in 1997 with Web-based access, but still on the old subscription model and using their aging closed interfaces. LEXIS/NEXIS and West remain almost entirely text based, and their private search tools are poor seconds to the Web's search engines. Much of these companies' actual data, moreover, are public data (laws, court opinions, and other government publications).

These competitors have been so focused on matching feature and function with each other, implicitly agreeing not to compete too much on price, that they appear to have completely missed the killer app coming right at them: the Internet's superior user interfaces and exploding public databases.

A number of completely innocent experiments now appear likely to obliterate the market for the closed services, right under the noses of the dueling giants. Cornell University offers a database of opinions from the U.S. Supreme Court that is not only free but much easier to use, search, and print. Government agencies, at the same time, are offering more and more of their information directly to the public (such as the House of Representatives' Thomas, the Patent & Trademark Office's database and searching tools, and the Securities and Exchange Commission's EDGAR system for company filings). It won't be long before someone takes these fledgling experiments, puts them together, and wipes out the information empires of both LEXIS/NEXIS and West.

There is a winning digital strategy for these information providers. Although they charge based on access, the real value they provide is enhancing the raw information they collect with commentary, indexing, and organized notes services. Instead of access, the companies could sell their expertise on a subscription or a transaction basis (for example, answering specific tax questions). Doing so would ultimately bring them into competition with their current customers, lawyers and accountants, but without the considerable markup the professionals add in answering simple legal and regulatory questions for their clients. LEXIS/ NEXIS and West are so comfortable charging for access and so convinced that their value is somehow inextricable from the closed networks and the mountains of paper they generate that neither has given serious consideration to this or any similar option. Indeed, the last time we spoke to both companies, they were still denying the existence of any serious threat from the World Wide Web.

A similar misfortune seems likely to befall the real estate industry, where buyers and sellers of houses and condominiums are actually kept apart, not brought together, by the closed multilisting systems maintained by real estate agents and brokers. These systems list only property offered by other agents, and are only available to the agents themselves. The agents protect the value of this closed system by agreeing to share commissions equally on sales—half for the seller's agent, half for the buyer's. Since there is no commission to share on unlisted properties, buyer's agents do not show properties that are not in the system, forcing buyers and sellers to use an agent whether they want one or not.

Agents, as we have said, generally provide value only to the extent that they reduce transaction costs for buyers and sellers. In the absence of other mechanisms for buyers and sellers to find each other and negotiate terms, the commission charged by real estate agents may have reflected a fair return on the service provided. Not anymore. In the rental market, several remarkable Web sites, like Visual Properties, walk users through the process of deciding what kind of apartment they want, what features they need, desire, or don't care about. These applications provide tenants with a list of available properties ranked by the tenant's own criteria, along with floor plans and virtual walkthroughs of the units. Applications, credit checks, and much of the administrative noise are automated and electronic. Soon, landlords and tenants will be able to negotiate in real time, face-to-face, using videoconferencing.

A number of interested parties, like Microsoft, Yahoo!, and Digital City, have strong incentives to build similar interfaces for home purchase and sale, a direct competitor to the real estate agents. These killer apps will make it easy for buyers and sellers to create their own real estate markets and to exchange much more information—including photographs, videos, and replicas of key documents—than the text-based listings used by agents. The new competitors won't need commissions, since they can derive revenue from advertising or possibly from the listing itself, as if it were a classified ad.

Real estate agents show no signs of seeing the coming threat, and consequently no signs of opening up their listing services or enhancing them to stay competitive. Once the killer app hits, we suspect they will find commissions are no longer a dependable source of income. Instead, real estate agents will need to figure out what actual value they still bring to buyers and sellers. Then they'll need to find a new way of charging for that value.

Giving Away the Store

Sometimes even organizations that make their living on open systems struggle with their counterintuitive behavior. Technology leader Hewlett-Packard recently found itself with this problem. The company had survived a devastating shakeout in the computer industry during the 1980s by focusing on open standards and architectures rather than proprietary ones. So HP was naturally disposed toward the Internet revolution when it occurred. HP was hooked on internal E-mail early on, and from the beginning of the Web's history has offered one of the best presales interfaces for customers wanting to search through its vast catalog of products and technical specifications.

Internally, HP also found that open systems were crucial to achieving reduced product development times, a key requirement for a company that relies on innovation and speed to maintain market leadership. The HP brand stands for customer responsiveness and superior engineering (as the recent commercial of a copier that does everything, including mowing the lawn, satirizes). Innovation has a practical benefit as well, since HP makes its best profit margin during the first 180 days after a new product is launched. After that, given the nature of open architectures, competitors start to catch up.

The natural tendency for HP was to open all its systems, including its product development processes, to customers. Customers were already involved in product development, and the collaborative technology had proven itself not only internally helpful but scalable to large global project teams. HP customers already had access to the Internet, so the financial cost of opening the interface would be minimal.

The problem was the very openness of the system. Inside HP and even with suppliers, it is all well and good for prerelease product information to be shared and worked over by as many people as possible. But if that interface were open to customers, the proprietary value of the data would quickly disappear. Opening the system, after all, creates a tremendous temptation for competitors. Once we open the fire doors that separate us from the world outside HP, a senior HP I/S executive told us, there's nothing to keep our chief competitors from discovering our plans for the next generation of products. And that would mean the end of HP's early advantage.

HP resolved the conflict in favor of broad, open access, in part by recognizing that some competitors were already inside the door. Canon, the chief competitor in the ink-jet business, is also the key partner in the laser-jet business, supplying the engines for these devices. Canon, in other words, already had access to much of HP's engineering expertise. HP realized that its own expertise was not so much in product innovation but in the *speed* of that innovation. Given the same product specifications, HP can get a new product to market consistently faster than its competitors. The risk of losing proprietary data, then, was less grave than the company initially thought. Put another way, much of the proprietary data turned out not to be all that valuable in the first place.

HP also understands, as the legal information providers and real estate brokers so far have not, that whatever value is lost from opening the interface and giving away information needs to be balanced by the additional value received. Including as wide an audience in the development, sales, and manufacturing processes as available technologies permit subjects that data to Metcalfe's Law, increasing rather than diminishing its usefulness. The bigger the network, the greater the utility. The moral of the story, and the general lesson of this rule, follows: Give away as much information as you can. Users give back more than they take away.

8. Structure Every Transaction as a Joint Venture

As killer apps squeeze out transaction costs, improving the competitiveness of the open market at the expense of large corporations, organizations must shift their activities accordingly. The business firm of the future will be a networked one, with technology providing partners with the needed communications channel that today might require an internal department. The concept of virtual organizations is now taken for granted, and the reality is rapidly approaching. GM, for example, recently sold Hughes Electronics, noting that it could get the same value through various alliances with an independent Hughes, thanks to digital technology. Ten years ago, access required ownership.

Davids versus Goliaths

Businesses all over the world are spinning off, selling out, and downsizing like crazy. These phenomena have been going on so long that it's more appropriate to think of them as features of the business environment than as trends. The restructuring of the corporation is a direct response to the new forces and the Law of Diminishing Firms. Firms get smaller when size isn't necessary or competitive. The new forces, led by the digitization of information, make it both possible and necessary to operate in smaller, more focused and more flexible units. Soon you will be able to treat basic transactions with the same attention you would a complex joint venture, bringing in the best set of business partners and allocating work, risk, and ownership as best suited.

A new breed of competitor is already following this rule, perhaps under your competitive radar. Entrepreneurs, start-ups, and the self-employed, who don't have infrastructures to dismantle, are taking advantage of inexpensive new technologies for collaboration as quickly as they are developed. Firms with no offices, no fixed employee bases, and no physical presence to speak of, are already making effective use of the Internet and related technologies to compete head-on with traditional firms. They're really not firms at all as much as loose affiliations of individuals with different skills who can use the low-transaction-cost digital marketplace to form and disband easily around projects.

Larger organizations must now learn to buy, sell, partner, and compete with a new breed of virtual firms, digital Davids in a world long ruled by Goliaths. In Holland, for example, the largest Internet access provider is not the national phone company but XS4ALL, a company started by a motley crew of former teenage hackers. By refusing to follow the business model of a telephone company, XS4ALL captured over half of the access market from the Dutch PTT in a matter of months.

The new forces will soon give rise to short-lived joint ventures that exist solely to complete one transaction, effectively replacing permanent organizations, long-term contracts, and strategic alliances. Competing against such firms isn't impossible, but it is certainly different. On the side of the traditional organization are powerful information assets like brand, relationships, and expertise, which, if properly digitized and optimally distributed, can form the basis of new competitive advantage. On the side of the Davids, however, is their lack of physical assets. They have no aging infrastructure or corporate bureaucracy, and lack the legacy of value-warping regulation. As one colleague of ours says, "A regulated economy creates a regulated mind-set," and the latter—as evidenced in telecommunications, defense, and the airline industry—seems harder to undo.

One industry that is already feeling the pinch of these stealth virtual ventures is the public market for capital. Heavily regulated at the national and state levels, the finance industry has turned its complex rules into barriers to competition. It limits the number of traders and the timeliness of information (the New York Stock Exchange requires its members to respect a twenty-minute delay in active quotes). Entrepreneurs hoping to raise money for new enterprises must engage a vast bureaucracy of underwriters, investment bankers, and lawyers, all of whom take a piece of the proceeds for their help in dealing with each other.

Andrew Klein, owner of microbrewery Spring Street Brewery, chose not to play by the rules and instead used the Internet to find the new business partners he needed to fund an expansion. Filing his own registrations, he cut out several layers of expensive intermediaries on Wall Street and sold $1.6 million in stock directly to 3,500 individual buyers. Klein didn't stop there. With permission from the Securities and Exchange Commission, the beer-maker launched Wit Capital in late 1997, an on-line investment service that will replicate the Spring Street experience for any company—or private investor—that wants to avoid the usual suspects in the securities market. Exploiting the dramatically lower transaction costs of cyberspace, Wit Capital and other Internet-based services are making it possible for complete strangers to form partnerships and finance new ventures.

Wit Capital is a good example of how digital technology can be used to build new relationships, using the frictionless flow of bits to smooth the transition from one organization's border to the next. But treating every transaction as a joint venture goes further. It requires an attitude toward interacting similar to the one in AOL chat rooms that focus on money and investing—you bring whatever valuable information you have, quickly determine who and what to exchange it with, and derive value from the sum of the parts. It is not who you know anymore, but what.

This is how the investors who use AOL's Motley Fool investment service claim they have been able to beat the market time and time again. One participant notices low inventory for disk drives at the local electronics store; another drives by the manufacturing plant late at night and sees a filled parking lot; a third reads between the lines of a press release. Combined, this information suggests an unexpected demand for product, and the investors predicted correctly a big run-up for the company's stock. The partners in this venture can each take the enhanced information and trade on it. They do business with each other based strictly on the value of their information, without lawyers, contracts, or articles of incorporation.

Partnership Portfolio Management

More than ever, the ability to form relationships and keep them healthy is a core requirement for any business, whether a large multinational corporation or a self-employed entrepreneur. As the distinctions between you and your business partners become blurred by the breadth, depth, and persistence of your connections, managing relationships becomes even more central.

The partnership range (see Figure 5.1) demonstrates the correlation between commitment and intimacy in an organization's connections. The choices range from basic awareness of the partner to outright ownership, as well as such interim arrangements as strategic alliances, licensing, joint ventures, and equity stakes. To design any killer app, you must hone your ability to identify potential partners quickly, determine the appropriate level of intimacy for the relationship, and secure the corresponding level of commitment with as little fuss as possible. Remember that competitors (and future competitors) are waiting in the wings, ready to move fast—maybe faster than you are.

The technology industry itself provides some of the best examples of winning and losing strategies. Microsoft quietly bought or invested in twenty companies in 1996 alone, at a cost of $750 million dollars, in order to gain early access to the nascent technologies these companies were developing. One company Microsoft purchased outright in 1997 was WebTV. Though sales of the WebTV devices (manufactured under

license by Philips and Sony) had been disappointing in the 1996
Christmas season, Microsoft paid $435 million for the company,
betting on WebTV's ability to develop enhancements that could
take the TV beyond computers in communication speed and
data storage. A few months later, Chairman Gates continued to
build his portfolio of related interests, buying a 25 percent
interest in cable TV giant Comcast after Comcast's chairman
dared him to prove that he really could make money in the trou-
bled industry. Many of these acquired technologies may prove
unmarketable, but Microsoft, like any good investor, knows that
it is the overall portfolio that counts.

Poor partnership management, on the other hand, can just as
easily be an organization's undoing. Consider the unhappy fate
of General Magic. This innovative company, founded by Apple
legends Bill Atkinson, Andy Hertzfeld, and Marc Porat, promised to jump-start the market for small handheld computing
devices by developing top-quality software to operate them.

FIGURE 5.1

Partnership Range

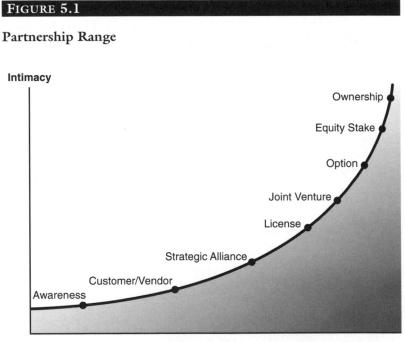

When the company's stock began trading in 1995, it raced to $28 a share, yielding a market capitalization of nearly $1 billion. The company had developed a powerful operating system and programming language for these devices, which it hoped would finally get the stalled hardware market off the ground. Even more impressive was the list of partners General Magic lined up to market its technology, including Apple, Sony, Motorola, Philips, AT&T, France Telecom, NTT, Fujitsu, and Matsushita. The partners were not only licensees but investors in the company. This unique coalition was formed in the hope of agreeing on a set of standards. Since all the major parties were represented on the "Founder's Council," there was no way General Magic could fail.

But it did. When we visited General Magic in 1996, the company was a shadow of its early exuberant self. It is now struggling to reposition itself as an Internet product and service company. The goal of creating and establishing standards had been blindsided by the Internet juggernaut and its open standards, in particular the Java programming language, which Sun had simply released into the Net. General Magic was so busy balancing the expectations of its partners that it completely overlooked the building momentum of the arguably inferior standards being promulgated on the Web. It was killed not so much by the killer app, but by the kindness of its investors.

Put another way, General Magic had failed to include a crucial partner on its Founder's Council: the user. As of late 1997, the current share price hovered around $1.

Summary

The new forces not only alter the nature of interactions between organizations but mandate a new breed of technology-enabled interfaces between you and your markets, customers, suppliers, and other business partners. Since functions now move fluidly to the place where they are best performed, interfaces need to be transparent and adaptable to their users. In creating these windows to your organization, you must be sure to choose designs that are appropriate for their users, even if they represent traumatic changes inside your own business. Rather than blindly characterize all of your organization's information as proprietary and secret, balance the true value of these bits against the potential for business partners to increase their value by using them.

Following these rules will take you into the world of the future, where transactions have already moved far along a spectrum from the carefully orchestrated to the purely ad hoc. The more open the system and the more refined your skills at forming, executing, and completing joint ventures, the better positioned you will be to exploit new opportunities, launch new products and services, and unleash your own killer apps.

Getting the rest of the way means remaking yourself from the inside out, the subject of the last set of design principles.

6

redefining the interior

Live in the future. It's happening now.
—The Firesign Theater

AS YOU EXPLOIT the power and ubiquity of digital technology, capitalizing on its ability to reduce transaction costs and create value-generating information products, severe pressure is applied to the organization you are today. Over time, old industrial structures fall away, and a new wired organization emerges. This event comes about not by means of planning for it but as the product of a natural and organic process. It is a function of the same forces that your digital strategy is shaping into killer apps. All you can do is help the new organization start to breathe.

The last four principles of designing killer apps, discussed in this chapter, focus on the creation of a new internal corporate self, one that is flexible enough to squeeze through the barrier between physical space and cyberspace. These principles are:

9. Treat your assets as liabilities.

10. Destroy your value chain.

11. Manage innovation as a portfolio of options.

12. Hire the children.

We start with the balance sheet, or rather the underlying business model it both represents and reproduces. Industrial cost accounting values the means of production (the trucks, the factories, the licenses) rather than the assets themselves; human capital, intellectual capital, and brand don't show up on the balance sheet. This kind of accounting looked right when competitors were effectively locked out without a physical plant; when, in other words, initial investments and operating costs of smokestack assets were the true barrier to competition.

The Law of Disruption changes the nature of these barriers, and the valuation of assets must change with them. Exposure to killer apps doesn't devalue physical assets so much as it reveals the disconnect between them and the actual production capacity of the firm. Lower transaction costs and low-cost technology help virtual competitors enter your markets with low start-up costs. When you compete in cyberspace, these asset-less firms often prove to be more nimble, flexible competitors precisely because they have few assets. What's more, they can generate brand of their own on an accelerated Metcalfe curve. They're not firms at all, some of our clients say, but just brokers, partnerships, and cherry-pickers, skimming off the most profitable customers, products, and channels. Thanks to the new forces, these *are* your competitors.

As the Law of Diminishing Firms operates, intermediaries in particular can no longer keep the link between the value they legitimately add and the commission they charge a secret, since everyone else on the chain (as well as everyone else *not* on the chain) can see the true costs. Long-standing, mutually supportive, and often implicit understandings (or maybe delusions) of each other's turf evaporate. An all-out information war is erupting in many information-intensive industries, with cheap technology as the ammunition. The battlefield is growing fast. Is that good news or bad? If you're the consumer, it's good news, because it turns out you were paying for a lot of inefficiently managed services you may not even need or want. If you're somewhere upstream, the answer depends on how fast you can rid yourself of underperforming assets and make the transition to value-based pricing.

As the operating model for your industry goes through major reconstruction, the last step is to get a lot smarter about planning and preparing for the next set of changes; even as you're replacing those permanent walls with modular units and trading today's expensive lighting, heating, and communications systems for digital alternatives, you need to begin planning for the day, which might come sooner than you think, when you won't have a physical office at all.

Such planning is rarely done today. Often, in fact, the staging and structuring of investments in future technology is given no attention at all. When it is done, most organizations demand that technology investments meet return on investment criteria, with detailed costs and benefits calculated in advance. We recommend something much closer to a portfolio approach, which includes a number of low-cost, high-risk, and high-potential options to spread risk and maximize coverage. Options valuation models are long established, and they are probably in place somewhere in your organization already. Now they must be adapted and used to create a new technology plan.

9. Treat Your Assets as Liabilities

Information providers, service firms, educational institutions, and even public utilities are struggling to become digital as quickly as possible. Doing so is hard for several reasons, not the least of which is the unsettling effect on your balance sheet. Organizations discover that the true value of their company is its information, but that value is now sunk into the various containers and equipment used to transform it from one good or service to another. Look at the annual report of a news organization and you'll see line items for printing presses and plants but not for expertise and intellectual capital—not, that is, for the organization's *ability* to generate, shape, and communicate the news. This is partly an accounting problem. Partly it is an attitude problem.

It isn't that the value of today's organization is disappearing so much as its form is changing. You must now rethink not only the value of the company's bits but also the true value of its atoms, some of which you may not need in the near future. It's important to shift your investment to bits, because those new competitors that have *none* of your fixed assets—no real estate, no manufacturing equipment, no distribution network—will suddenly look competitive in the new business environment. Your assets become liabilities.

This reallocation of value is happening on a broader scale as well, as the physical infrastructure of the overall marketplace is being replaced by a virtual market, or what Harvard Business School professors Jeffrey Rayport and John Sviokla call the marketspace. Because trade has until recently required a place where buyers and sellers could come together to safely exchange their goods and money, markets originally developed where there was good access to transportation and communications. Waterways and roads led to the creation of warehouses and factories. Urban centers continue to be the hub of commerce today where people still need to interact to complete transactions. But as commerce sheds its physical form, the need for the marketplace diminishes. This is not an evolutionary change, like the development of futures markets (which did away with the need to bring actual goods to the sale), but a revolutionary change. The Law of Disruption is eliminating the need for any physical marketplace.

Some organizations may turn out to have no information assets, or at least none that can't be quickly eliminated by a stroke of the deregulating pen or introduction of a killer app. As Nathan Myhrvold, Microsoft's chief technology architect, points out, banks (at least commercial banks) may soon be wiped out by the widespread use of digital money, which provides a superior alternative to cash, checks, and credit cards, and which could be offered just as easily by nonbanks (Myhrvold is thinking of his own organization here). Cash and other financial instruments are technologies created by governments and banks to reduce the transaction cost paid by buyers and sellers to exchange the value of their transaction (my goat for your land, my loyalty for your frequent-flier miles), and that transaction cost is rapidly falling as information flow improves.

Newspapers may be in similar trouble, since they rely on classified ads for up to 80 percent of their revenue. In their printed form, classifieds are nearly unusable compared to new digital forms offered in various city guides (Yahoo!'s and Digital City, for instance). Digital ads can be automatically searched, delivered, and linked to their advertisers, who can in turn test and target their ads with pinpoint accuracy. The New York Stock Exchange, real estate brokers, and many of today's television networks may find themselves similarly out of an industry. As the CEO of a large investment bank described his own situation to us, "Why does anyone need an investment bank or broker? Well, probably because he either doesn't have enough information or he does not have the means physically to execute what he wants to do. Technology is giving him the information and the means to execute. This disintermediates a lot of people in my business."

The Reincarnation of Printers

Not everyone is afraid to face the cold hard truth about their disappearing assets. Financial printing, a $1 billion specialty industry that prints millions of pages of securities-related filings for public offerings and quarterly reports, looks on the surface like an industry seriously at risk of disintermediation. It took its first big hit in the 1980s, when the need for typesetting and photographic plating, once high-margin components of document preparation, declined as desktop publishing software became available on even the least-powerful home computers.

In 1995, the Securities and Exchange Commission dropped an atomic bomb, announcing that starting the following year, companies could begin filing electronically through its Electronic Data Gathering, Analysis, and Retrieval (EDGAR) system and avoid much of the need for printed reports. The killer app for financial printers had, it seemed, arrived.

The industry has not disappeared, however. Instead, it has flourished. Financial printers recognized quickly that competitors in the electronic filing market would need no fixed assets, and that this lack of assets would be a benefit rather than a hindrance in the new world. The printers responded quickly by aggressively going after the electronic market themselves, capitalizing on their long-standing relationship with the securities industry to obtain a first-mover advantage.

The strategy is working. Bowne & Company, one of the industry leaders, submitted almost 15 percent of all EDGAR filings in the first months that electronic filing was authorized. In total, financial printers were responsible for over 40 percent of the first electronic filings. Bowne has also expanded its capabilities to publish not just on paper but electronically and on the World Wide Web. Rather than quietly be eaten alive, the industry has embraced digital technology and used it to expand.

Financial printers, it turns out, are not their equipment. They are organizations with substantial expertise in the ins and outs of complicated government filings, the discipline to work under tight and exact deadlines, and a reputation for carefully handling highly confidential information. They have a brand. These are the assets that printers like Bowne are trading on in the digital world, not the equipment that shows up on their balance sheet. The ability to distinguish the two may very well mean the difference between surviving and disappearing.

The Threat to Heavy Industry

For manufacturers and heavy industry, we suspect, the idea of outsourcing production and distribution activities seems ludicrous. But the threat of losing competitiveness by failing to realign assets is very real. In our work in the chemicals industry, we have already observed the emergence of a new breed of information companies, such as ChemConnect, which are building virtual markets for consolidating and trading on transactions that today are the private dealings of one buyer and one seller. These brokers, which have no fixed assets, can collect price and inventory information over the global information network and use it to coordinate the buying and selling of bulk and even specialty chemicals, activities they perform over the Internet. They are using technology to reduce transaction costs, and doing so as a new, information-intensive intermediary.

Perhaps over time these brokers will themselves be replaced by more automated markets, operated by software agents like those being developed by Firefly, Jango, and others. Today they threaten manufacturers where it counts—on the bottom line. By forcing a wedge between buyer and seller with superior information, these brokers have the potential to extract significant margin from all transactions, forcing producers increasingly to a commodity price set for the minimum profit. Information advantages have provided protection from such intermediaries in the past, but that time is coming quickly to an end. The information is nearly all there now, and those who can exploit it first will win.

This is not just the case in chemicals. Telecommunications brokers have been buying and selling communication bandwidth in bulk for years. The same thing will happen in power and energy, and it has already occurred for oil and gas. (Providence, Rhode Island, for example, recently switched its energy supplier to a buying consortium that does no generating of its own.) In these industries, producers and refiners have responded to the threat of information brokers by focusing more on specialty products, reducing costs with new technology, or by taking on the brokering function themselves. But to do so requires tremendous flexibility, flexibility that aging infrastructure and the mindset that goes with it make difficult to achieve.

For one large chemicals company, we helped develop a digital strategy that fights fire with fire. To cut off the emerging information brokers, the company is developing a rich "information pipeline"—modeled on the physical pipelines it has been building for almost fifty years—between itself and its customers and suppliers. The new pipeline would replace the ad hoc channels of communication that already exist, such as telephone, mail, and Electronic Data Interchange (EDI), a limited computer-to-computer communications protocol that allows basic information on purchases and invoices to be transferred. The pipeline is based on the open standards of the Internet, the equivalent of EDI raised to a power of ten.

Using digital technology to reduce inventory and duplicative handling (another transaction cost) has been the theme of cost savings in other industries, particularly retail sales, but our client's approach leapfrogs even these impressive developments. The information pipeline will enable the company to offer customers a virtual inventory of finished products, thereby reducing its own inventories for generic and specialized products without adding any risk of insufficient supply. In effect they plan to create the illusion of a build-to-order environment, a value-added service that encourages loyalty to the producer. In reality, with access to the requirements of all its customers, the producer could largely continue producing to stock.

On the other end, the suppliers, especially those from whom it purchases large volumes, can manage virtual inventories for the producer with equivalent savings. In both cases, the producer is fighting commoditization by adding new value. And in both cases, that new value comes from information, all of which has been available but waiting for suitably cheap and ubiquitous technologies to be useful.

What should you do? By now you should have a good sense of how your own industry is changing and where you stand relative to your current competitors and business partners. You should also have identified which of your current assets are most at risk, if by no other method than imagining how new competitors can use digital technology to compete against you without these assets. Use that information to begin the shift to a more digital existence, perhaps outsourcing some of the depreciated functions as an interim strategy.

10. Destroy Your Value Chain

A value chain, as we said in Chapter 3, is the series of functions that create and distribute an organization's goods and services. Along the way, transaction costs, both internal and external, add up. Throughout the book we have given examples of industries in which overall value chains, including interactions with upstream suppliers and downstream customers, are coming under severe pressure from the disruptive power of the new forces. In fact, we know of no industry in which the phenomenon isn't going on to a greater or lesser extent. Rapidly changing rules and shifting allegiances are the most visible symptoms.

Many organizations are preemptively destroying their own value chains. Recognizing that change is coming that will obsolete their infrastructure, force them into a commodity role, or remove them from the process altogether, many are choosing to hasten the end of the old model. They use digital technology to break the rules, implicit or explicit, dictating how buying, selling, or producing goods and services is done, and form new relationships with customers and competitors by automating expensive processes, or giving away proprietary tools others can use to evolve away from the industry entirely. The hope of these organizations is that by unleashing the killer app themselves, they will be able to exert some control over how much earth is scorched in the process.

One of our clients is in the business of selling home heating oil, a part of its larger oil and gas retail operation. It is a depressingly difficult business. They sell to a deeply fragmented market, in which our client controls 17 percent of total sales for its market area but only 4 percent of direct sales to residents. Sales to residents, ironically, generate 75 percent of its profits. Sales to independent local dealers are made at much lower profit margins. The company's brand name is not strong, and it is limited by restrictions from its parent company in how far it can expand into new markets and products. Almost 70 percent of its customers are over the age of fifty, suggesting that home heating oil is a shrinking market. Exit costs, finally, are too high for the company to simply walk away from the business.

This, in an odd sense, is the good news. The prospects are so poor that the company has very little to lose in breaking the industry rules and purposefully destroying its value chain. The company has decided, therefore, to expand direct selling to the residential market, even though doing so will very likely upset the independent dealers. And they are adopting this strategy despite the fact that dealers currently have the advantage of personal relationships with customers, more flexibility on terms and delivery, and lower distribution costs.

Rather than compete with the independents on their own terms, the oil company has designed an entirely new business model, which it calls the Virtual Fuel Company (VFC). Once complete (there are several interim stages), the company will physically exist only as the producer of heating oil, handling the remainder of activities through partners or virtually in cyberspace. In the early stages, customers will be given the opportunity to order over the telephone or through the World Wide Web, but the longer-term plan is to connect sensors in the home heating oil tanks to the production facility over a wireless network or through the home's connection to the Internet. The VFC will then tell the customer when it is time to refill rather than waiting for an order. And delivery logistics will be coordinated through partnerships with leading transport companies already serving the VFC's markets, which have plenty of excess warehousing and transport capacity. The VFC will route pickup and delivery schedules to the transportation companies' systems based on its projected sales.

Advantages of the new model for our client are obvious. The company will not need an expensive sales or distribution function because they will outsource order processing to the customer. The supply and distribution network will be virtual. And the company can use their new information channel with the customer to form alliances on matters of mutual interest, such as environmental and regulatory issues. All this will make it possible to compete aggressively with the local dealers on price, at the same time reversing the advantages of location and personal relationships the local dealers have today.

Each of the advantages for the company translates into added convenience for the customer. In addition, the system will allow the VFC to provide better sales and service than the independents as well as other valuable information such as maintenance schedules for the customer's equipment. Instead of the very limited hours during which the parties can transact today, the VFC will be available to its customers, for information or deliveries, twenty-four hours a day.

. . . Or Someone Else Will

In the case of the Virtual Fuel Company, a disadvantaged player already in the industry decided to solve its problems by wrecking the business model for everyone. It remains to be seen if this company can maintain the will to complete its strategy and what moves its former customers (and new competitors) will make in response. The market for home heating oil in the VFC's market, in any case, will never be the same.

More often, it is a start-up or an organization from an entirely different industry that will decide to destroy your value chain. These new entrants have even less of a vested interest in the old model and often can do much more damage much more quickly. Companies focused on competing in the current market often overlook these new players, dismissing them and the technology they employ as insignificant until it's too late to respond strategically.

In 1995, Amazon.com launched the first virtual bookstore on the World Wide Web. Started by investment banker Jeff Bezos with money he borrowed from his family, Amazon became "Earth's Largest Bookstore" by mid-1997 with a remarkable inventory of more than 2.5 million titles—most of them maintained for Amazon by its sales and distribution partners—any of which could be delivered within a few days by delivery partner UPS. By mid-1997, Amazon had sold books, tapes, and other media to more than 340,000 customers in more than 100 countries, with revenues of $16 million in 1996 and easily double that in 1997. According to Bezos, his start-up, Internet-only company already generates the revenues of twenty-eight big-chain superstores.

Amazon, like the Virtual Fuel Company, followed many of the design principles stated here in unleashing this killer app, including the destruction of the existing value chain. Its competitors, bookstore chains like Barnes & Noble and Borders, who have themselves been busily rewriting the rules of book retailing formerly dominated by independents, maintain expensive storefronts in hundreds of locations and supply them through an elaborate distribution system that includes warehouses, trucks, and gigantic inventories of books. Amazon, which operates only in cyberspace, has turned all of these advantages into disadvantages. Even though it has no stores, its customers can shop anywhere at anytime they like. And because 60 percent of the books it sells come from a single wholesaler, Amazon's inventory and handling costs are minimized, while the customer still gets home delivery within a day or two. Amazon passes much of the savings on to customers, offering an unheard-of 40 percent discount for its most popular 500 titles. Soon, the company plans to ship some orders directly from their partners' warehouses and expand their own warehouse to further streamline order fulfillment.

Amazon is using the unique properties of its technology interface to improve the admittedly unexciting experience of shopping and buying books electronically. Its Web site, which is constantly updated, provides easy-to-use search tools, automated E-mail messages announcing to customers new books of interest, and a search service for out-of-print books using the Internet. Amazon is also establishing a community of value by giving readers and authors a forum in which to post their own reviews and comments on the books in its catalog. The company plans to host real-time discussions with authors. These experiments may evolve into a collection of microcommunities of interest, an infinite number of specialized, ad hoc, global book clubs.

Amazon had no competition from the traditional players for over a year, even though Amazon's approach to retailing posed a threat to the big-chain bookstores' value chain at several vital links. Afraid of cannibalizing its own expensive bookstores, Borders has yet to provide a virtual service of any kind, and Barnes & Noble went on-line only recently. (In an ironic gesture pitting the old world against the new, Barnes & Noble filed suit against Amazon on the same day it launched its Web site, arguing that Amazon's claim to be "Earth's Largest Bookstore" was false advertising, since Amazon didn't *physically* have the books.) Amazon had a year in which to develop its own brand—a cyberspace year, the equivalent of seven years in the physical world—and the traditional booksellers will now need to match Amazon not only on price but on the features that have made Amazon's interface unique.

Death of the Middleman

Examples of organizations destroying their own value chains so far have come from companies at either end—companies, that is, that produce goods and services or that distribute them. What about everybody in the middle? As we mentioned in Chapter 2, this is the group that is the most vulnerable to the Law of Diminishing Firms, since their value is based on the existence of transaction costs. As these costs decline, so does the need for intermediates. One of our clients, a division of a global transportation giant, specialized in expediting cargo between European countries based on expertise in various import and export rules and regulations. The business disappeared one day in 1992, when Europe dropped its borders.

Middlemen are perhaps the most vulnerable to the killer app that disrupts today's industry structure. Pity the warehouser whose retailer customer decides to distribute directly to its customers using package delivery partners. Pity the bookkeeper whose job it is to consolidate financial information that the bank decides to offer as a free electronic give-away. The death of the middleman has been a theme sounded by the academic and business trade press for years. Dire predictions have it that everyone from brokers to handlers, expediters, lawyers, wholesalers, and warehousers, as well as travel agents, insurance agents, and other remarketers, will eventually be cut entirely out of the picture, or "disaggregated." But in many sectors these intermediaries have proven to be remarkably robust. Long chains are being taken apart, but they are also being put back together in new configurations. To paraphrase Mark Twain, reports of the death of middlemen have been greatly exaggerated.

What's going on? We have worked with several traditional middlemen and come to the conclusion that dramatic changes are transforming but not destroying the business of many intermediates. Wholesalers and others have been operating in a largely static environment for some time, and part of the problem is that there is a serious breakdown between what intermediates do and how they charge for their services. For convenience, most intermediates charge based on commissions, percentages, or markups to the goods they handle. Producers and retailers eager to improve their own profit margin are determined to eliminate as many of these charges as possible. What many seem to forget, however, is that middlemen are more than just what their name suggests. They add value to the goods and services that pass through their trucks, warehouses, consolidations, and so on; it's just that the connections between the value and the fees charged have been lost.

Now, thanks to the new forces, they must be found, and middlemen, like everyone else, will need to inflict serious damage to their current business models to exploit them successfully. Local markets are turning global, and retailers can now form relationships with a rapidly-growing assortment of international suppliers. Using digital technology, they can do so at low cost without the need for wholesalers. Warehousers are similarly threatened by an increasingly efficient, ever-growing global package delivery network, driven by cheap computing, large-scale data networks, global positioning satellites, and other outputs of Moore's Law. Agents of all kinds, with their physical overhead and corresponding geographical limitations, are suddenly having to compete with electronic agents that can surf the Internet on a customer's behalf and find the best possible deal.

On the other hand, the collapsing value chain creates opportunities as well. Intermediates can also establish a global presence and can begin to offer their services to a wider range of customers on a greater scale. The nature of the services, however, must change. We believe, and our wholesale clients agree, that the concept of "wholesaling" will soon disappear. Instead, today's wholesaler will need to take a cold hard look at current activities and extract from them the valuable skills and other information assets that it can begin offering outside the traditional industry structure. Wholesalers will become financers, logistics specialists, outsourced pre- and postsales support providers, and more. They need to wrap information around the products they handle, adding measurable value in the process. As one client from the travel industry put it, "Add value or adios."

11. Manage Innovation as a Portfolio of Options

Organizations unleash killer apps when they combine ideas, digital technology, and the will to change. We'll talk in Part 3 about generating the ideas and finding the will, but what about the technology? Where does that come from? How does a FedEx or Charles Schwab even know what Internet-based customer interfaces are possible and when to upgrade them with new media? How does the Virtual Fuel Company know that wired fuel tanks are a likely option in the near future? How did financial printer Bowne & Company learn how to develop Web sites and format electronic filings?

In most organizations that we are familiar with, investments in innovation almost always follow a conservative model. Up to 90 percent of I/S funds are spent developing and operating current systems, most of which run on older or even outdated technology. Of the 10 percent remaining for research or technology advancement, another 90 percent may be spent studying technologies that are almost mature, like the next release of Microsoft Windows or application suites like SAP. For developments that are more than 18 months from commercial use, there is usually no activity, except for the kind of skunkworks investigations that a field manager might perform. Yet Moore's Law and Metcalfe's Law guarantee that innovations will be arriving and achieving critical mass during that time.

The problem is a mismatch between investment styles and investment instruments. At a recent meeting of the Diamond Exchange, executives described their investment strategies. At best, investments in innovations are justified using rolling five-year plans and the exacting business case approach of return on investment (ROI). If projects cannot guarantee satisfactory returns, they are not funded.

While this approach is appropriate for incremental efforts, it can't possibly work for investing in new technologies, new ventures, or in innovation generally. How can senior management, let alone I/S professionals often untrained in either finance or strategy, hope to estimate the benefit of a technology that doesn't even exist in the form of a good or service? How can you calculate the return on investment of an experiment that could destroy your value chain or turn assets into liabilities? At the same time, no responsible manager would simply toss financial analysis out the window and throw research dollars wildly at new ideas, hoping that something will stick.

The key to this deadlock has already been mentioned, and it is the approach of technology leader Microsoft and venture capital's Kleiner Perkins Caufield & Byers. These firms invest in dozens of promising technologies and developments, not as an owner but as a stakeholder. Taking a small stake keeps the exit price low for investments that fizzle, leaving the possibility for a dramatic upside—killer app upside—for investments that do pay off. By diversifying the innovation investment, the 10 percent of the I/S budget set aside for research could be managed not as a series of discrete projects, but as a *portfolio*.

Portfolio management, using the tools of risk analysis rather than ROI, has been the byword of venture capitalists for years. These financiers have not only made their investors rich but have driven the innovation powerhouse of Silicon Valley to become the preeminent source of economic growth in the global economy. Now it's time to follow their lead with your own funds.

Tim Andrews and Jay Kingley, partners with Diamond Technology Partners, developed this new approach to innovation management. Both Andrews and Kingley spent part of their careers as senior executives of technology start-ups, where they learned firsthand how investors cover their risk of loss by hedging, taking options rather than ownership, and spreading risk over a number of promising technologies. Rather than looking for specific ROIs, the "option-creating initiative" (OCI) weighs the option price, strike price (the price to turn the option into full ownership of the technology, or a bigger stake), and volatility of the investment against the potential value of the option. Options serve to decrease uncertainty about the value of the underlying transaction, a powerful tool given the uncertainty-generating potential of the Law of Disruption.

In addition to the new discipline of risk analysis, which ensures regular and frequent evaluation of the portfolio, OCI requires a working mechanism for abandoning options that fail as quickly as possible. According to Andrews, "The exit strategy forces corporate leadership—not the project team—to revisit regularly the decision to let the option lapse, or to exercise, turning the experiment into a full-scale product development."

Even an organization as venerable as the British Post Office has learned the value of operating a miniature venture capital firm within its I/S department. In 1997, the Post Office's executive committee created an innovation fund to give business managers a way to experiment with technology pilots and trials without being trapped in the business case morass of the regular budget process. Successful proposals must satisfy two of three evaluation criteria. They must (1) deal with a technology wholly new to the Post Office, (2) propose a creative new application, one that has the possibility of becoming a new service, or (3) involve a substantial technical or business risk.

With seed money of 4.5 million dollars a year, the fund received over thirty proposals in its first six months of operation. The first project to be approved is a pilot for improved vehicle navigation systems for postal vehicles and will include experiments with global positioning satellites for navigation, collision avoidance technology, and real-time congestion reporting. A one-day meeting convened to launch the innovation fund drew more than 200 executives. As the Post Office's experience shows, there are plenty of ideas floating around in every organization. People just need an opportunity and a forum to express them.

The Story of Lotus Notes

David Reed, former chief scientist for Lotus Development Corporation and now a technology investor himself, recently told us the story of how the OCI approach worked for the development of Lotus Notes, a software product that allows organizations to create collaborative work spaces over local and wide area networks (and now the Internet as well). Notes was released in 1990, when Lotus's chief product offerings, the 1-2-3 spreadsheet program and the Symphony suite of related products—themselves killer apps—had largely died out. Notes became the company's principal source of revenue until 1994, when IBM acquired Lotus for $3.3 billion, a price that largely reflected its valuation of Notes.

Ray Ozzie, a talented programmer who had designed Lotus's Symphony product, came up with the idea for Notes in late 1984. Ozzie wanted to develop a new approach to sharing information among PC users in a group. "In those days," says Reed, "the idea sounded totally off the wall. PCs had barely penetrated the market. Local-area-networks (LANs) were just starting and it was not obvious what they were good for. E-mail had been heavily used by programmers in DEC and Software Arts, where Ozzie had worked earlier, but Lotus did not use E-mail at all. Windows 1.0 was a cute idea, but a technical dog, and Ray's product idea depended on the multitasking capabilities of Windows. There was no market case for such a product, and most people could not imagine why anyone should care."

Nonetheless, Ozzie believed that the idea would take off once a critical mass of networking applications and PCs with the power to support graphical interfaces and multiple applications running simultaneously were available at reasonable cost. Lotus founder Mitch Kapor shared that belief, but neither could say when the prerequisites would be met. There was no sensible way to make a business case for investing the resources it would take to develop the Notes concept sufficiently to decide whether it was a winner or not.

Kapor, a leader as well as a visionary, found a way to keep Ozzie involved with Lotus. The solution was a new investment model that aligned the interests of both parties while managing the uncertainties of the Notes project. Kapor formed a new corporation called Iris Corp., which was founded solely to develop the Notes concept into a product. The structure of the transaction was unique. According to Reed, "Lotus was committed by contract to fund the development of the product, but Lotus did not own the product. Instead, Lotus had the right to review progress periodically and decide whether to continue funding the project. As long as Lotus continued to fund the project, Lotus had the right to take the product to market at the point when it was ready. If Lotus stopped funding the project or decided not to bring it to market, Iris was free to take the product to market by any means it chose, including working with another company, such as Microsoft."

Between the time the project was initiated and the time Lotus brought Notes to market five years later, there were many inside Lotus, Reed says, who felt that the investment in Iris was a bad idea and urged Lotus's senior management to cut Iris's budget. "Typical questions raised were: 'Why are we wasting some really talented people on a wild goose chase?' 'Before we cancel project XYZ, shouldn't we look at the money we're pouring into Iris?' and 'What does Iris have to do with our strategy?'" Unlike other projects, however, Iris had a contract in hand that gave it leverage in such discussions. Their leverage, however, was limited to the value Notes had outside of Lotus— if the project really had no value to the market, then Lotus could easily drop its funding. "As a result," Reed says, "Lotus was highly motivated to invest resources to learn how to bring Notes to market in the most effective way. If the best possible analysis determined that Notes had no value, then Lotus would suffer no remorse at writing off its sunk costs."

After several years and multiple senior management reorganizations (including the departure of Kapor), an entrepreneurial manager brought the product to market, and after a shaky start in 1990, Notes gradually evolved to become the centerpiece of Lotus's strategy and the basis for IBM's hostile takeover in 1994. Says Reed, "I'm convinced that had Notes been handled as a 'normal' internal development project, the pressures to apply the best talent to short-term crises, plus the uncertainty about when the market would materialize and what the demand would be, would have caused Ray and his team to be reassigned, and the project would never have happened. Or, alternatively, had Notes become known as the 'chairman's pet project' it would have been overprotected and would not have had the close scrutiny that it did receive, resulting in a much more polished product and positioning when it was finally introduced."

Managing innovation as a portfolio of options, as these stories suggest, requires new skills. It also requires leadership and will. As we will explain in Chapter 7, the disruptive power of digital technology alters the roles and relationships between I/S executives and the rest of the management team in many ways. From the standpoint of innovation, senior executives must now be involved in technology investment decisions. They must take ownership of the portfolio and manage it, as Mitch Kapor did, as if the future of the organization depended on its paying off. Because it does.

12. Hire the Children

Young people, especially children, implicitly understand digital technology in a way that the rest of us can only watch and admire. John Perry Barlow calls them the "natives" of cyberspace. MIT's Andy Lippman makes the point even more poignantly. Speaking to a large European industrial company struggling to understand how it could turn itself into a digital-ready company, and fast, Lippman said there was only one way: "Hire the children."

Tomorrow's customers, competitors, and business partners, born and raised on digital technology in their homes, schools, and toys, will not only expect but demand commercial relationships that are technology enabled. Children who grow up playing with 64-bit networked video games won't simply reject text-based interfaces and suboptimal communication speeds, they will find them incomprehensible, like some form of hieroglyphics. And their attention spans for new goods and services are themselves expressed in Internet years—that is, they are about one-seventh as patient as adults.

The good news, however, is that today's children will be the product designers, customer service providers, and business managers of tomorrow. One way to understand the needs of the next generation is by talking to them and creating an environment where they can build the structures that will take today's organization forward. You can succeed at digital strategy, quite simply, by putting them in charge.

Organizations need not wait for tomorrow's managers to grow up before they can begin to learn from them. A recent *Business Week* article on the potential benefits to child development of extensive video game play told the story of a demonstration by network game company Total Entertainment Network to senior computer simulation experts from the U.S. Department of Defense. The company's CEO was trying to demonstrate how to play Quake, the hugely popular game that has taken over the Internet gaming world, and failing miserably. As it happened, the thirteen-year-old son of one of the meeting's organizers was in the room. He took over the keyboard and blew away all of the CEO's opponents.

MIT sociologist Sherry Turkle has made a formal study of the changing way in which children respond to technology. Following on the classic work of child development expert Jean Piaget in the 1920s and 1930s, Turkle has been watching children use technology to form order and structure in their universe, creating theories about space, time, causality, and life. She began this work in the early 1980s, but in the 1990s, Turkle writes, she found that children's response to computers, in particular, had changed significantly. "[C]hildren still talk about computers as 'just machines' but describe them as sentient and intentional. The very notion of a machine has been reconfigured to include an object with a psychology."

Turkle tells the remarkable story of a thirteen year old playing SimLife, a sophisticated game that simulates the life of an ecosystem the player designs. The child is clearly unaware of much of what was going on in the game. After Turkle asked repeatedly if the game's confusing messages bothered him, the child sought to reassure the adult: "Don't let it bother you if you don't understand. I just say to myself that I probably won't be able to understand the whole game any time soon. So I just play."

It isn't just children who are different, but young adults as well. We recently took a group of twenty executives from different European postal agencies on a technology tour of Silicon Valley and stopped in for a day at Rocket Science, a game company headquartered in San Francisco's growing multimedia neighborhood. The oldest employee we could find was well under forty, and the environment clearly reflected a generational difference in attitudes toward work. The executives were amazed at the work styles they saw—people everywhere, running in and out of each other's offices, holding impromptu meetings and resolving problems as they came up. There was no sign of bureaucracy or authority and little structure to the work or the work space. Yet it was clear that Rocket Science's game developers were working with tremendous energy and productivity.

Most remarkable of all, as an I/S officer from the British Post Office observed, was the attitude of Rocket Science's employees. "Everyone is smiling," she said. "They actually seem to be enjoying themselves." She thought about that for a moment and added, "They're not working, they're having fun."

Creating work environments like Rocket Science—environments suitable for children—isn't easy. As the CEO of a major banking organization told us recently, "How do you change a culture from one of hierarchy with the normal pyramid to an open, flat culture where the 25-year-old kid can say to me, 'You're crazy. That won't work. Where did you get that dumb idea? We have to do it this way.' And I willingly sit there and listen to him?' "

Hiring the children—or including them in the process of product development, strategy formation, and workplace design—is the easy part. What is more difficult is learning to see through their eyes and trying, as best we can, to live in their world. But that is the only way, in the end, to develop a process that sustains the discovery, formation, and unleashing of killer apps.

At a recent workshop on digital strategy we conducted for an international management consulting firm, we began by giving two ten year olds (the children of some of the participants) each an unopened box containing a Sony PlayStation. The PlayStation is a powerful game computer with more raw processing power than most high-end desktop computers that cost thirty times as much. We asked them to put it together, connect it to a television and start playing with it, which they were able to do in less than ten minutes. Along the way they described what they were doing. "Now, this is the CD. I don't really know how this works, but you need it to play different games."

While we started our speech about the power and unpredictable nature of killer apps, the children drove three-dimensional race cars across the Golden Gate bridge, projected on screens behind us. The children were so absorbed by the game that they soon forgot they were standing in front of an audience of adults, and one of the parents tried to quiet the children lest they interrupt the presentation. No, we said, don't stop them. Their joy in playing the game was precisely the point we were trying to make.

This last design principle brings us full circle, since we began by talking about the need to think more about our dealings with business partners, including those business partners—our employees—with whom we transact the most business. The next generation of managers, laborers, and CEOs are the children of Moore and Metcalfe, born under the sign of the Law of Disruption and uttering Ronald Coase's name, figuratively, as their first word. This group already controls a sizable chunk of the economy, and that chunk is growing exponentially along with Moore's Law. So now is the time to introduce yourself to these mutated creatures, otherwise known as your own children. The sooner you can incorporate their values and their energy into your organization, the more likely you'll be remembered by them with some emotion other than nostalgia. They might even admire you.

Summary

The final four design principles round out the key techniques organizations are using to implement their digital strategies and design killer apps of their own making. Here we have stressed the necessary evolution that moving to cyberspace will require of your internal organization—your market, your assets, and most importantly, your people. The rehabbing and reinvention of the corporate self in many organizations will require trauma equivalent in force (but faster in velocity) to the movement in the nineteenth century from an agrarian economy to an industrial one. Much of the change will occur as a natural by-product of responses to the new business environment described by the first eight design principles.

We have left many questions unanswered. How do companies utilize the design principles in practical terms? How do they make themselves ready for a new strategy, generate ideas, and operate the emerging new business in a way that maximizes the potential for future success while preserving today's cash flow? How, in short, do they learn to unleash killer apps in practice? That is the subject of the next part of the book.

unleashing the
killer app

THE FUTURE ARRIVES so quickly that the designers of Disney's Tomorrowland have given up. They can't build an environment that doesn't look stale before it's opened, so they've decided to go backwards. Gone are the rocket ships to Mars, the House of Tomorrow, the PeopleMover, and the Carousel of Progress. The new Tomorrowland looks like a nineteenth-century fantasy of today, heavily cribbed from Jules Verne and H. G. Wells. It's a "classic future environment," as Disney puts it, tongue firmly in cheek.

The new forces have given all of us a chronic case of future shock. Individuals, so far, have proven themselves to be pretty adaptable, but what about organizations? As the market becomes more efficient, and does so more quickly than organizations, how can you break the mold and turn the future from a threat into an opportunity?

In Part 2, we presented a set of principles designed to drive planning in the digital age. Applying these principles will help to identify killer apps that take you out of the past and into the future. To succeed with digital strategy and to be able to unleash killer apps continually, you've got to go further. You need, as David Reed says, "to live in the future, not just visit it." Living in the future means making digital strategy your operating model—the strategy must be so well integrated into the culture of your organization that it becomes indistinguishable from manufacturing, distribution, marketing, sales, and administration.

In this third and last part of the book, we describe how organizations can make the transition from digital strategy explorers to integrated digital enterprises and, in particular, how the role of senior executives changes in the process. We begin by taking you inside two organizations, one a leading consumer brand and the other a large industrial conglomerate, to see how the process of developing a digital strategy worked and didn't work the first time through. We then describe the process these two organizations followed in more general terms.

As a framework, we present the seven-step process used by Diamond Technology Partners (see Figure 3.A). In the context of this process, the early charter of a digital strategy project is to

FIGURE 3.A

Exploring and Exploiting the Digital Future

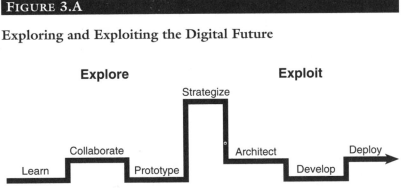

Source: Diamond Technology Partners. Reprinted with permission.

teach the organization how to think about its future, including the experiments with technologies and partners it must begin today. We describe how organizations start the process by discarding old organizational baggage about the proper role of technology and partnerships. We also prescribe a series of readiness activities that raise senior executive awareness, placing digital strategy squarely and permanently on the executive agenda.

7

digital strategy
in practice

*You can no more reason from highway precedents to railway prob-
lems than you can reason from the ox to the electric battery.*
  —Brooks Adams

You do not need to understand electricity to use it.
  —Julia Cameron

TIM GALLWEY, best-selling author of the "Inner Game"
series of sports instruction books, has spent the last fifteen
years applying his techniques to business settings. When he
talks about the learning process, he uses words like "awareness," "commitment," and "trust," words more common
in Zen than in business. Through a series of clinics and
workshops, Gallwey teaches executives how to discover the
obstacles that get in the way of performance, and to rescue
themselves from the inner voices of self-doubt that inhibit
their learning.

  To succeed at digital strategy, your organization must be
a learning organization, more focused on ideas and experiments than detailed plans and forecasts. The change is not
as dramatic—or weird—as it first sounds. Organizations are

at their core learning entities, reinvented over and over again throughout their history. Without a learning capability, the organization would never have come into being, and if the need to change is ignored for too long, the organization will perish as surely as if it was denied capital, employees, and markets. That, as Ronald Coase might say after taking one of Gallwey's clinics, is the nature of the firm.

Organizations that practice digital strategy must learn to communicate with their organization's change center. The language it speaks is the language of ideas, scenarios, options, and what-ifs. In this chapter we tell you the story of how two of our client organizations learned to understand and speak this language.

Two Giants, Two Missions, One Approach

The clients are fast-food industry leader McDonald's Corporation and German industrial powerhouse VEBA AG.

McDonald's, one of the most recognized brand names in the world, has expanded at an impressive pace throughout its history, spreading not only its products but its commitment to value, convenience, and a dependable customer experience. McDonald's customers know that they will be served good-tasting food quickly and courteously and at the lowest price possible, whether the restaurant is in Kansas City or Kuala Lumpur.

VEBA, less well known in the United States, is Germany's largest conglomerate, with total revenues of more than $42 billion a year. Founded more than a hundred years ago as a government-owned corporation involved in coal mining and processing in Germany's Ruhr Valley, the company is now a diversified conglomerate, including divisions that are leaders in electricity, chemicals, oil, transportation, real estate, trading, and wholesaling. VEBA owns Germany's second-largest electrical utility, PreussenElektra, and a few years ago began preparations for the deregulation of the German telephone market by creating a new subsidiary, OTELO, in cooperation with RWE, its chief competitor in the electricity business. VEBA's objective for OTELO is to challenge the current monopoly or near-monopoly of Deutsche Telekom in everything from residential and business phone service to cable television and corporate data networks.

As these brief introductions suggest, the future holds different challenges for these two companies.

McDonald's goal is to continue its expansion on a global basis and, if possible, to accelerate the process. In 1995, the company opened new outlets (including mini-locations inside convenience stores, gas stations, or temporary storefronts) at the rate of more than 2,000 per year worldwide, nearly double the number opened in 1993. At the same time McDonald's is increasing its scale, the company is pursuing several operational strategies:

- Improving the company's ability to provide customers with value, based on competitive price, food quantity, overall experience, and the like.

- Improving information flow between stores and the marketing organization so as to move quickly in markets where price and tastes (responses to promotional items, for instance) change rapidly.

- Finding ways of operating the stores at the lowest cost but with the highest commitment to a consistent, high-quality experience for customers.

Each of these strategic initiatives is supported by full-time I/S resources, and McDonald's CIO Carl Dill decided to revisit each of them through the lens of digital strategy. Though each strategy supports several systems initiatives, Dill was concerned that the I/S teams were too reactive and might be missing opportunities and overlooking risks that didn't appear on their radar screens. He was also aware that separate technical architectures for networking, data exchange, and processing, although optimal for the individual strategy, would fail in the end to give McDonald's a flexible, open base on which to build in the future.

For VEBA, the overall challenge identified by CEO Ulrich Hartmann is the transformation of the holding and its subsidiaries from industrial companies to an integrated information-age enterprise. Hartmann and his corporate planning department are well aware of the new forces and how each of them is already affecting VEBA's traditional operating model and asset base. In utilities, as we mentioned, European integration will eventually bring competition for PreussenElektra, and the trade and transportation units feel increased competitive pressure from the rapid globalization of their activities (globalization largely enabled by technology). VEBA itself has already taken the lead to compete through digitization by launching and investing millions of dollars in its telecommunications start-up.

In launching the digital strategy project, Hartmann tied the overall goal of his organization to the successful integration of technology. As a former mining company, VEBA understood the metaphor of "mining its bits," and it has plenty to mine. Each subsidiary has expertise and customer data that could be of considerable value to the others, but for organizational and technical hurdles that blocked the flow of information. Data sources are disparate, and the subsidiaries had developed a culture of independence (based in part on incentives to do so that came from VEBA's reporting and financial evaluation criteria) that made cooperation difficult.

So Hartmann formed a digital strategy project team, led by his corporate planning department and supplemented with outside assistance from the MIT Media Lab, consultants from CSC Index, and ourselves. The goal of the project was to identify threats and opportunities from digital technology that would be difficult to see from the perspective of VEBA's corporate culture. The project's findings were a major theme of a spectacular meeting of all VEBA managers in 1996, a two-day event in re-unified Berlin, which Hartmann called a "meeting of the minds."

Tapping the Vein of Gold

The key objective of the digital strategy projects at both McDonald's and VEBA was to invent the future. To do so, we started by playing with it. In meetings, workshops, and short projects, we used the twelve design principles to imagine scenarios of how the companies could change their industry and their own positions within it. These were not necessarily destinations anyone would actually reach; in fact, some were abandoned early on. But having some destinations in mind is more helpful than having none.

In this work, the focus is not on technology and what it might be capable of doing for us or to us. Rather, the goal is to paint a picture of what the organization wants to be doing with its time and resources in the future. This could be based on a strategic plan and what the plan established as the stretch goals for the organization, or it might be inspired by a review of what partners and competitors are doing (or not doing). The goal might also be the product of brand-new ideas, pulled out of thin air, based entirely on the collective imagination of those involved.

Every organization we have worked with has found its own way of conducting these brainstorming sessions. One organization had teams of executives play the role of well-funded outsiders, both new entrants and existing competitors, and asked them to devise business plans that attacked the organization's prime markets and stole away its most profitable customer segments. Knowing the blinders of the organization, and the exposed flanks of its offerings, these teams easily put together alliances and business propositions that realistically challenged the status quo.

In some organizations, the process captures the imagination of a much larger group. In the early 1980s, Apple Computer produced a high-quality videotape inspired by a remarkable device that had been dreamed up by Alan Kay, which he called the Dynabook. The video showed life in a near-future where computing on small, personal devices that kept track of appointments, placed video conference calls, and looked up data from computers all around the world had become ubiquitous. We still show this tape to companies having trouble looking past their own four walls, even though much of what Apple imagined has now arrived.

American Express's customer service department, similarly, produced a video demonstrating a brilliant reconception of the entire service function and how technology could change it for the better. These included learning interfaces that would give customer service representatives relevant history and make recommendations for additional goods and services to offer the customer while he or she was on the line. The tape generated tremendous excitement within American Express, and while the company itself largely failed to follow through on the most promising ideas, many of them are now standard features of the sophisticated customer service functions of catalog sales and home shopping companies.

A videotape is just one way to document a vision, and nothing that elaborate is required. Details are not important. Practical reality and the laws of physics are also unimportant. What is important is coming up with one or more powerful ideas about what the organization should look like in the next five years, including ideas that contradict each other. Later, you'll figure out how and whether you can actually get there.

Rethinking Strategy at McDonald's

Large or complex organizations usually need to break the planning process down into manageable units. McDonald's developed its future scenarios around three strategies—customer convenience, customer value, and optimal operations. For each of these strategies, there was already a full-time team that included both operations and systems development personnel from Carl Dill's organization. The digital strategy project team worked through these teams to generate the bold new ideas that Dill instinctively knew were there to be discovered.

First, the digital strategy team reviewed the current plans of each of the three teams and developed an initial list of new and emerging digital technologies that might play a key role, for better or worse, in realizing the teams' strategies. In assessing the strategy aimed at improved store operations, the digital strategy team noted a possible mismatch between the identified projects and the overall direction of the company. The operations team had characterized the stores as miniature manufacturing facilities. Consequently, it was working to improve the suite of manufacturing systems—inventory control, production planning, financial control, and point-of-sale order entry—that supported the store.

But Cindy Elzinga, the digital strategy team leader, wondered if the more appropriate model for McDonald's future might not be that of a service company. After all, the stores already offer considerably more than hamburgers and french fries. They serve as a family retreat, where parents can relax while children play with promotional toys or in increasingly elaborate indoor playgrounds, and as a community center for senior citizens, who in many locations are invited to the stores to play bingo. A large part of the reason people go to McDonald's is the community that it fosters.

Assuming this trend would continue, Elzinga believed that the operations team should expand its initiatives to include more service-oriented technologies. Could McDonald's offer computer games instead of and more cheaply than plastic toys? Could the experience in the stores actually be enhanced by replacing human order takers with learning interfaces? Could more food production processes be automated, freeing up in-store personnel to interact in more interesting ways with customers? If so, what technologies should the team be considering now that it was not? How carefully had the stores team reviewed developments in multimedia interfaces, interactive television (order in advance from home or the car?), robotics, and modeling and simulation tools?

Similar analyses were done for each strategy, after which the digital strategy team held a half-day workshop with all three teams. Where possible, key technology partners and vendors of the newly identified technologies were invited to participate. The strategy teams each gave a brief presentation of their major initiatives, after which the digital strategy team began pushing the new ideas and technologies.

We asked each of the three strategy teams to imagine and describe what the business would look like were the team to achieve its wildest goals. With the customer convenience team, one of the key initiatives was to improve the speed with which new stores and new kinds of stores could be opened, and the result of the workshop was the development of a "day in the life" scenario for site developers that described the optimal toolset and collaborative environment they would have with them as they scouted locations.

Rather than choosing individual tools from separate vendors today, we asked the convenience team to think about the tools on the horizon—geographical information systems, global positioning satellites, new media such as video and teleconferencing, and the expanding information flow of public networks such as the Internet. Didn't the differing pace and divergent platforms of such technologies suggest that the longer-lasting toolkit would be one built for easy swap in and swap out of tools? It would be a mistake to lock in to a platform that could support only a subset of today's options and, perhaps, none of tomorrow's.

For the customer value team, the focus was on real-time information flow that would allow for instantaneous corrections of the menu and prices to respond to customer preferences, the competitive environment, and even the global commodities market for ingredients. How far was McDonald's today from having that kind of information? How close could it be if it invested in available technologies? What would it take to get the company all the way there, and who would they need to work with to get there faster, and first?

After these meetings, the digital strategy team sifted through more than a hundred pages of detailed notes highlighting the ideas that had provoked the most response—positive or negative. In addition, the team identified what Carl Dill had referred to as a superset of "agility" imperatives that each strategy team needed to include in setting its individual agenda. These imperatives were the themes that had raised the most promising new technologies that might otherwise have been missed.

All the teams, for example, needed to begin thinking about the implications complete information would have in the near future. How would their goals change in a world where each transaction—including purchasing, pricing, menus, and site development—could be customized in real time? A second of these stretch goals was to design every system in the context of

Moore's Law and to recognize that the need to scale up (a local system becomes global) and scale down (a global system becomes local) was a necessary component of every systems initiative.

Hosting a Meeting of Minds at VEBA

At VEBA, the natural organization for the project was along major lines of business. The digital strategy project team performed a brief competitive assessment of the business line's use of digital technology as compared to industry leaders in other countries, then held a workshop with the senior management of the affected subsidiaries. The goal was to develop a general model of the competitive pressures that were soon to enter the picture as a result of new technologies, deregulation, and the opening of markets to other European Community countries. The workshops included not only the team's analysis of the industry pressures but live demonstrations of the way organizations from around the world were already using digital technologies in creative ways that addressed (or aggravated) the problems.

These workshops were carefully prepared by the corporate planning department and representatives from the executive team of each subsidiary. The executives' major concern was the company's possible complacency. Given the excellent overall performance of VEBA on a sustained basis, the executives intuitively believed that they were not sufficiently worried about the future. They asked the digital strategy team to try its best to challenge this mindset. In short, they wanted to be shocked and surprised. The team decided that the best way to do this would be to take the executives on a trip to the future, which, in other industries or markets, had already arrived.

For the retail group, this included live demonstrations of electronic commerce over the World Wide Web, and for the real estate holding it meant demonstrations of multimedia CD-ROMs that showed how easy it was to design lifelike virtual tours of everything from gardening techniques to the Louvre. With the trading subsidiary, the team demonstrated developments in virtual reality software that could make simulated product selection and configuration so lifelike that it might eliminate the advantage of local agents and consequently wipe out a major investment of the company.

From these exercises it became clear that each business line was threatened by the rapid arrival of the future, including pressures animated by the technologies themselves. In each workshop, the presentation and the ensuing discussion focused on a likely set of new industry models and a series of interim roles and solutions the organization could participate in to ensure a positive outcome. The "output" of the visioning process itself was simply the minutes of the discussion held during the workshops. At least that was the tangible result. More importantly, however, the process triggered the beginning of a series of major ideological changes within the organization—not only in terms of attitudes and approaches to digital technology but to the very ideas of planning, competitive analysis, and strategy.

The focus of the project team shifted to learning how the business line could preemptively respond and thereby shape the future environment to the company's own best use. For each business, a series of projects was defined that included short-, middle-, and long-term options. In many cases, the subsidiaries agreed that the way was clearer than the will. Executive teams began to rethink and realign their relationships with I/S resources, and several subsidiary CEOs made public their intention to take responsibility for new technology introduction or to begin to experiment with technologies that were already on line in other industries or markets, particularly in the United States. One subsidiary CEO decided to create a digital readiness group, whose chief would report directly to the CEO.

The attitude of each subsidiary to the holding company and to the other subsidiaries began to change as well. Initially, each subsidiary requested its own private workshops, but at each the digital strategy team raised questions about how partnerships across VEBA could help the different parties achieve common goals more quickly and effectively. Organizational barriers, some extremely long-standing, began to relax, and multicompany workshops began in earnest. Corporate planning staff from the holding company were invited to participate more freely in subsidiary activities, and the holding's role of coordinator and community builder took on new meaning. These developments, as Hartmann had planned, culminated in the Berlin "meeting of minds" in June 1996, where many of the CEOs included future technology plans in their presentations and information booths.

Gold on the Floor

The development of a digital strategy is not a linear activity. It is not about going through a long, deliberate process of business analysis. It is not about whittling the list of possibilities down to the one big initiative that everyone must then salute. Once the flow of ideas gets started, they often come in a flood. Some ideas come out in extremely embryonic form, but others, perhaps interim solutions, emerge fully formed. When they do, there's no reason to be bound by the methodological mindset that says they must go into a queue and wait their turn. That's why there is an innovation portfolio.

At McDonald's, advances in public networks and the availability of information had been underestimated, so the company slowed its deployment of a private satellite network to reconsider the value of this proprietary system. At VEBA, it was clear that electronic commerce was a key threat and opportunity that spanned all subsidiaries, and some experiments had begun even before the initial digital strategy project was complete. These early results are like gold lying on the floor of a mine.

Another client, describing his own experience evaluating emerging technologies, referred to these as the "painfully obvious" solutions. Once the organization sees them, it's hard to understand how they stayed hidden as long as they did. The pain came from his recognition of the fact that he could have been developing new customer interfaces, offering new digital goods and services, or forming powerful electronic links with business partners much sooner. The technology was there, the opportunity was there. But the planning processes and atmosphere for innovation generally filtered them out before he had a chance to see them.

For VEBA, it was clear that what was most needed was a mechanism for communicating information between the companies. Consequently, a corporate intranet was quickly planned, implemented first at the chemicals subsidiary. VEBA is now expanding it to cover the entire organization. At McDonald's, the weakness of the company's technology radar became painfully obvious, and the I/S organization corrected the problem with a dispatch appropriate to the company's customer service model. The team developed a list of "painfully obvious emerging technologies" and for each reviewed what evaluation and experimentation initiatives were under way in the company. In some cases, more resources were added; in many others, this was the first time the company had any first-hand experience with the technology.

Whenever we work with clients in developing digital strategy, as at McDonald's, a small subset of emerging technologies are quickly identified as being crucial to the future of every strategy or business unit or both. The sad part is that in nearly every case, when we then look through the organization to see what's currently being done about these tools, the answer is often nothing. Senior executives don't take the emerging technologies seriously and the information systems professionals don't have any information on them. Nobody is paying any attention to them.

The short-term solution is obvious: Do your homework. If you're very uncertain about a technology you know is very relevant to your business, you better start learning about it. If global communications is key to your future strategies, you need to get smart about global communications networks and the Internet. If electronic commerce is the way you're going to salvage current markets in the next years, or take yourself global, don't close your eyes because electronic commerce hasn't matured yet. Start figuring out what's missing that you need. Is it digital payment? Widescale access? High bandwidth communications? Adequate security? Trials for every one of these future applications are going on right now, and you should consider being a part of them. If not, you should at least follow the progress of those who are.

A list of "painfully obvious" partnerships will also emerge. As with the critical technologies, we recommend you stop and take a look at your relationships with all the business partners who appeared over and over again during the digital strategy workshops. If it's the top 1 percent of your customers, what kind of relationship do you have with them today? Do you even know who they are? Do you give them any reason to believe they play a key role in your future? If you have determined that the only way to avoid disintermediation is to forge highly robust links with your upstream suppliers, what are you doing about that today? Do you give them access to your E-mail, voice mail, and other critical systems? (If you don't, do you think there's some reason they'll give you access to theirs?) Is the relationship with key technology vendors in the hands today of the I/S department or, worse, the purchasing department?

Lessons Learned from Practice

There are a few additional lessons to be learned from the stories of McDonald's and VEBA as both companies continue to refine and implement their digital strategies. At McDonald's, the project suffered from its origins as an I/S initiative. Carl Dill's courage and commitment are considerable, and the project had some visibility with senior executives. Visibility, however, is not the same as ownership, and the categorization of the project as a technology initiative rather than a strategic one made it difficult for the team to communicate the new ideas or develop them fully with their operations counterparts. Absent the kind of practical benefits senior managers were used to seeing for technology projects, the effort stalled.

At VEBA, Ulrich Hartmann knew before the project began that organizational and even cultural obstacles would be found, but perhaps not in precisely the manner and places where the team encountered them. The project team discovered, for example, that VEBA's telecommunications start-up was having trouble forming partnerships with the other subsidiaries, a problem now corrected by a clear mandate from CEO Hartmann that raised visibility at senior levels.

The solution overall at VEBA has been to focus the efforts of the corporate planning function. Corporate planning took a leadership role in the development of the digital strategy for VEBA, and it has continued to carry the torch with full-time commitment. It is championing the breakdown of information barriers inside the company and encouraging as broad a channel for communication as technology permits. The holding has begun development of an ongoing, continuous, and virtual "meeting of the minds."

Unleashing killer apps requires not only a process for transforming ideas into experiments with testable hypotheses. As the lessons learned by McDonald's and VEBA suggest, it also requires the ability to execute, to implement, and to make permanent the new openness to ideas and information exchange that are experienced during the project. What is required is to move digital strategy from a project to an operating model, the operating model of the future. The next two chapters describe how organizations are making the transformation.

8

redefine the problem

You cannot wait for an unguilty tool.
—Joseph Beuys

WE SAID IN Chapter 6 that one of the principles for unleashing killer apps is to manage innovation as if it were a portfolio of stock options. But how do you amass that portfolio? How do you pick the technologies and partnerships that will feed your experiments in developing killer apps? How do you know where to look in the first place?

This chapter is devoted to answering these questions. We will describe how organizations create a technology radar, feed a technology pipeline, and pick and choose the investments and partnerships that maximize their ability to develop and implement winning digital strategies. The commitment made to these learning and collaboration activities cannot be a one-time event, like an annual corporate retreat. The process is ongoing. It requires regular attention from senior management if it is to be kept alive and well. You can't turn the radar on only when you want something to appear in your range, nor can you maintain a relationship by acknowledging its existence only when it's convenient for you. You need to be present, in some sense, all the time.

Succeeding at these early stages of digital strategy development requires substantial changes to the organization. In particular, it requires a new attitude toward technology itself. You can't build a wired organization if you still believe, like many of the executives in our digital strategies survey, that technology is essentially a tool to implement strategy rather than the basis of forming strategy. You can't unleash killer apps without aligning senior executives and I/S professionals with the new, common goal of unleashing killer apps. You can't live in the future without moving there first.

There Is No Strategy without Technology

Competitive analysis in the new world is not done in the context of current market forces but rather in the context of the new forces, particularly digitization. Strategy work, and even reengineering work, has always had a technology component, but in the old world technology was where you went *after* determining the strategy. The project teams we worked on in the 1980s usually finished their work before they even made contact with the information systems professionals, and then only to start the *danse macabre* of trying to match future "requirements" with systems "solutions" based on mature technologies.

In the new world, you start with technology. Instead of being problem-pull, the new approach is also technology-push. What's more, you not only need to push technologies that aren't mature, but ones that have barely started gestation. Thanks to Moore's Law and Metcalfe's Law, those are the technologies that *will* be available when you implement your digital strategy.

New simulation tools, for example, may inspire an interior design company to leverage its expertise by developing software that lets customers do much of the basic design work themselves. It might then sell the product in addition to the hands-on consulting work it already performs. That software may in turn put stress on the services of lower-cost designers, who in turn may look to the Internet to improve their ability to source materials for their customers.

Developing digital strategy, as this example suggests, requires components of both problem-pull and technology-push. When the two are operating together in a well-functioning organization, the processes become not only circular but indistinguishable, creating what Philip Otley and Paul Spence of Andersen Consulting call a virtuous cycle.

The virtuous cycle is a pragmatic, indeed opportunistic, response to the new digital business environment. You explore future visions by looking at your business and markets through the lens of the twelve design principles, and then look at digital technologies that could most influence the development of those futures. Having identified some target technologies, the process then goes the other way, and you ask yourself how those technologies, in combination with others, might develop in ways that make your design goals possible or impossible. Or you can reverse the process. The process quickly moves from back and forth to a kind of conversation, where you integrate what you've learned about both perspectives. As you do so, the beginnings of new business options for your innovation portfolio—some the complete opposite of what you may have intended for yourself—begin to emerge.

The Do-It-Yourself Retail Exchange

In our work with a large European do-it-yourself (DIY) retailer, we began with the company's strategic goal to gain dominance in a highly fragmented market. Management believed the company had developed a powerful brand name and wanted to leverage that brand as it launched a significant expansion of its outlets. The digital strategy project team visited a few of the stores, however, and found that they were not appealing places to shop. Salespeople were hard to find and harder still to get help from. Some stores did well, but only because they were in good locations.

The retailer's original goal had been to find ways of improving brand awareness and value by doing a better job of placing its stores, improving inventory and service, and opening many more locations. The virtuous cycle process altered the direction of the planning. As the group reviewed developments in and examples of emerging retail possibilities of new media such as CD-ROM catalogs, electronic commerce, 3D interfaces, and real-time communications, it began to rethink the value of the company's physical assets. The discussion turned to the possibilities of expanding and improving the brand not through physical locations but through virtual presence.

For a wide variety of items carried by the stores, it was immediately clear that electronic shopping could be more convenient, could deliver a better customer experience, and could result in significant cost savings for both customer and retailer. While it was true that no one was likely to go to the Internet to buy a nail, they might well do so for a more expensive power tool. Or they might buy a package containing all the materials necessary to complete a project that was designed with an on-line simulator.

The question of what was most convenient inspired the management team to do something very interesting: they stopped the discussion and asked themselves a series of fundamental questions, some so basic that they might not otherwise have been considered: Why do people shop at DIY stores in the first place? Why had they grown so popular? Why was the market expanding? What features of store designs made one location more satisfying to customers than another?

To find out, the project team went not to the stores themselves but to cyberspace. In this lower-transaction-cost environment, communities of interest had been forming that could give the team some answers. The World Plumbing Council, a not-for-profit group, had created a remarkable site called Plumbnet, in which individuals post plumbing problems they are experiencing (for instance, "water leak somewhere between meter and house"). The software allows other users to post suggestions and to engage in an asynchronous discussion to solve the problem. Another site, Barter Systems, revealed the consumers' interest in avoiding what they perceived as overpriced contractors in favor of trading services with each other.

These and other demonstrations suggested that DIY was less a retail concept than it was a lifestyle. DIY stores seemed to have inadvertently tapped into a pent-up demand from consumers who wanted to do things themselves because they liked to and because they wanted to save money. DIYers, the project team concluded, are a disorganized community in want of not only supplies but a forum in which to trade information and barter expertise. Often they come to the store hoping to strike up conversations with other shoppers for that very reason.

So the recommendation the team made was to shift the strategy from a traditional market share approach to something entirely different—the goal of creating a community of value for DIYers. This was a need so poorly understood that no retailer had begun to address it, and we believed that whoever did it best could find themselves at the center of a wide variety of valuable transactions. Building the community center could distinguish the retailer as something entirely different, making the customer's trip to the store an experience rather than a transaction. And that, the team realized, could really do something for the brand.

The process shifted back to technology again, as the team looked for ways to destroy their existing value chain and cannibalize their physical stores by building this new concept with bits rather than atoms. The new virtual store was dubbed the "DIY Exchange." Sketches of the interface were drawn, and the company immediately began to look at how it could begin offering some goods and services on the World Wide Web to begin its collaboration with customers.

Ultimately, the team understood, the DIY Exchange had the potential to be a killer app, one that would alter not just the competitive landscape but the company's operations. Once fully implemented, the DIY Exchange would make retail locations look more like warehouses and showrooms than points of sale, and the electronic "store" less and less a reproduction of its physical counterpart and more like a network, connecting customers, suppliers, distributors, and contractors to each other, creating a virtual do-it-yourself community.

Operating under the virtuous cycle approach liberated the creativity of the digital strategy process. The retailer suspended its normal rules of engagement, which included long-term budgeting and detailed business case development for any new business investment of this scope. Instead, it essentially structured a business option. With a remarkably small budget and a volunteer team, the company began to experiment with the new model. Within a week it had met with its advertising agency, and within two weeks it had developed a user interface and a business model for offering some of its products electronically over the Internet. Within a month it was ready to pilot the first prototype of its Web site, an electronic catalog that included electronic payment and delivery services using its own stores as the distribution center.

Technology Alignment

As the DIY example suggests, organizations cannot unleash killer apps until they can harness their own business and technology expertise. We recently participated in a two-day workshop sponsored by a major European manufacturer to explore new ways of doing just that. This meeting, which included a miniature trade show of technologies the organization did and did not use, was attended by more than sixty people, including the CEO and the senior executives of most of the business units, outside experts, and about twenty individuals who identified themselves as I/S professionals.

At the beginning and end of the workshop, the participants answered a series of questions using an electronic voting system, and the results were displayed on bar graphs at the front of the room. The answers revealed a serious rift in the organization's attitudes. When asked "How much time and effort do you invest in developing your own information technology skills?" more than 20 percent of the I/S professionals said that they spent little or no time. When asked how significant a role technology played in the company's overall performance, more than 65 percent of non-I/S senior managers answered "critical," while nearly 50 percent of the I/S professionals answered "irrelevant."

Even at the end of the workshop, during which the CEO, among others, repeatedly stressed the critical role digital technology would play in the company's efforts to restart growth after a long period of cost cutting, 30 percent of the I/S professionals still said technology was irrelevant, and 30 percent defiantly maintained that they didn't plan to invest significant amounts of time in their technology skills. Almost 45 percent of the *non*-I/S professionals, in fact, were willing to commit themselves to spending more time developing technology skills than did those whose job it was, presumably, to lead the charge.

Whatever else these findings reveal about the health of the organization, it is clear that there was a serious communication gap between the I/S professionals and their operational counterparts. And, pretty typically, it was the I/S professionals who, in the voting and throughout the course of the meeting, expressed the most skepticism about the potential for new technologies to play a strategic role in the organization's future.

Unfortunately, many organizations have experienced a painful breakdown of goals and objectives as seen by the business and its I/S professionals. It's a problem not just in traditional businesses but even high-tech companies. About a year ago we heard from some colleagues who were working with the I/S department of a leading manufacturer of Internet hardware and software. The company was reconsidering its policy of forbidding the use of E-mail for any corporate business, which it had initiated in fear of having proprietary information intercepted. Did we know of any experts on encryption the client could talk to? Yes, we said, we knew the world's leading authority. As it happened, he worked for the client, in the same facility as the I/S department. Unfortunately, we said, he responds only to E-mail.

The reasons for these breakdowns are legion, and they have been the subject of numerous books. We think the basic problem is a historical one. Data processing functions began life in the

1960s as support departments, often in the development of back-office financial systems. In recent years, some companies have made significant progress in upgrading the status of this group to recognize its role in the basic operation of the business, and in many organizations there is now a chief information officer who reports directly to the senior executive.

Even so, attitudes do not change quickly. Today's senior executives were bred in a culture that insisted on engineering and business discipline and predictability from an I/S field that was too young to provide it. In many organizations, this led to dramatic disasters in terms of projects that far exceeded time and cost budgets or, worse, that failed altogether. I/S professionals, as a result, have been conditioned to work only with the most proven and mature technologies and to avoid technology risk taking (hence the old saying that no one ever got fired for recommending IBM). Everyone, including and perhaps especially the I/S professionals, became risk-averse.

As technology moves from its position as a defining element of the back office to a disruptive force in the marketplace, the problem now faced by most organizations is that there is rarely anyone, much less an organization, with the mandate and the resources to help senior management treat digital technology strategically. Before starting down the path to digital strategy, the organization needs to re-create the role of the I/S function, to give it and the organization as a whole a future- and growth-oriented technology mandate.

Aligning technology and strategy is not easy. The challenge is to build the kind of technology awareness infrastructure we described above and put technology not just on the organization's agenda but at the top of it.

Technology Radars

Part of the failure to use digital technology strategically comes from a simple failure to understand what the technology does. Asked about possibilities for using the Internet, the CEO of an investment banking firm reported that his company "had a, what do you call it, a page on the Internet, an address, or whatever, for six months and, at last count, we had 9,000 to 10,000 whatever you call them. I think we've yet to have our first trade." Despite the fact that his company's site didn't even *offer* an electronic trading option, he felt confident telling us that "We're not going to do anything of value on the Internet."

The single most important feature of developing a digital strategy is for everyone involved to see technology in the context of the new world. Unless you are in one of those rare organizations—a FedEx, Charles Schwab, Mastercard, or Hewlett-Packard, or a start-up like Security First Network Bank, Firefly, or Amazon.com—that instinctively understands the competitive threat and competitive advantage of the killer app, a key task in forming your digital strategy will be learning to integrate emerging digital technologies with current and future business operations. You'll know you're there when, like the companies listed above, *it becomes impossible to determine where the business stops and the technology starts.*

One of the best ways to accomplish this change, and one of its key outputs, is to launch a radical new process for raising technology awareness in the organization. Rather than waiting for killer apps to hit them over the head or, worse, wipe out current assets, channels, and customer bases, managers must learn how to recognize early potential and take appropriate steps to learn about, experiment with, and, if appropriate, exploit new technologies.

Organizations that have already implemented successful digital strategies invariably nurture a zealous, rigorous, and organization-wide technology radar that allows them to do just that. The technology radar is the pipeline that feeds digital strategy, and it must be operating smoothly and continuously if you have any hope of maintaining a competitive advantage. Before you can develop your strategy, you need to get this engine running.

The technology radar is only as good as its inputs, or, as the old computer saying goes, garbage in, garbage out. It is therefore critical to make sure you're pointing your sensors in the right direction. The focus must be on those digital technologies that, though not yet at critical mass from a commercial standpoint, are nonetheless ready for inspection and experimentation.

Too often we find that organizations track only mature or declining technologies and mistake incremental improvements to these applications for the true killer apps coming from left field. Companies focused on developments in distributed mainframe computing in the 1980s missed the PC revolution happening right in their own backyard; companies that are today focused on the next release of SAP, Windows, or the next level of Pentium processor from Intel are likewise missing out. Going on around them are the transformation to scalable network computing, heralded by the Internet; the development of platform-independent software environments like Java; and the revolution in computing devices that come not from traditional manufacturers but from consumer electronics companies. If you can't see the technology that's coming, how can you hope to exploit it?

Feeding the Pipeline

Once you've taken off the blinders, identifying emerging technologies and their future application is easy. Pick up any newspaper or magazine that *isn't* explicitly focused on technology, and you'll find stories about how digital technology is changing the world. Walk into any electronics store, new car lot, or toy store, and you'll see the applications that will be ready for business tomorrow (or sooner). Some of the best information on new technology is delivered using the technology itself, like Netscape's In-Box, which allows you to subscribe to a wide variety of news sources that are delivered in the form of customized multimedia E-mails.

Finding information is *too* easy. Finding useful information, on the other hand, is what separates success from failure. Identifying the emerging technologies that may be of actual value to the organization requires a fat pipeline, a sensitive radar screen, and a sophisticated intelligence function. Given the speed that new applications can climb up the Metcalfe curve, your view must be far-reaching and deep, but to survive the onslaught of available data, you'll need the triage skills of an emergency room doctor.

One of the most effective techniques for identifying new technologies and their developers (an equally important point, which we discuss a little later) is to take a periodic technology study tour, either virtually or, better yet, in the real world. We mentioned earlier a tour we designed for a group of executives from leading European postal agencies, including the British Post Office. The Post Office understood that personal communications—its core market—had already gone through significant digitization. It knew that its ability to survive and continue providing a useful service would be determined by its ability to understand such developments and take a leadership role in exploiting them.

The tour for the postal agencies progressed, like Joseph Conrad's novel *Heart of Darkness,* by moving from familiar to increasingly strange territory. After a day each at AT&T and the U.S. Postal Service, the group relocated to Silicon Valley. There the Europeans met the development team at Sun Microsystems that had launched Java, participated in the production of a television program about new technology at the studios of ClNet, and learned about the trials of developing virtual reality interfaces for the Internet from the twenty-eight-year-old CEO of a start-up whose product had been demonstrated the day before by Bill Gates.

At the end of each day, the members of the group met to debrief and put what they had seen into context. Discussions continued through dinner and well into the night, as managers and I/S executives found common ground, perhaps more so than ever before, in trying to make sense out of the future they were seeing. Maureen Gardiner, who heads development for the Post Office's Future Markets Group (and the woman who was so struck by how much fun the employees of Rocket Science had at work), took a group of her own for a second tour and then decided to get in on the fun herself. She has been developing a prototype Web-based mall for specialty catalog companies that will be hosted by the Post Office (which already delivers the goods), a nice example of managing continuity for her customers at the expense of her own organization's disruption.

Kicking the Tires

Having identified technologies or applications still in an immature form which you think may have some application to your future business, the most important thing you can do is get it in front of as many people as possible. You can talk about the Internet for hours, but get the CEO of an organization to spend ten minutes surfing the World Wide Web with the mouse in his or her own hand, and the potential uses begin flowing. Write all the reports you want about the value of three-dimensional modeling and simulation, but you'll have much better luck just giving everyone a copy of today's best software games.

We sometimes put together technology "discovery zones," where clients are encouraged to play with the products that could be the basis of their wildest dreams or worst nightmares. At a recent meeting of the Diamond Exchange, we immersed our executive members in a slew of alternative Internet access devices targeted at consumers, not business. The president of a major book publisher installed a WebTV straight out of the box (in ten minutes) and surfed Web travel guides for an upcoming vacation in Germany. The CFO of a major retailer, who had little experience on the Web, was able to find cross-country race results for his son's high school using a Sega Saturn. Everyone in the group saw themselves in cyberspace on a site that featured digital pictures uploaded in almost real time with a Casio Cassiopeia handheld PC. As our colleague Gordon Bell, a senior researcher for Microsoft and a venture capitalist, says, "A demo is worth 1,000 pages of a business plan."

Done in the right context, introduction activities create a rich environment for brainstorming, developing prototypes, and conducting other business experiments critical to developing strategy. We recently made a presentation to the managing committee of a leading Swiss bank, whose members had been told by their I/S department that it was too soon to invest much time or effort in the Internet. Using a laptop computer and a modem in the bank's own boardroom in Zurich, we bought and sold stock over the Web using software from Charles Schwab and E*Trade, both of whom charge less to clear trades than it costs the bank—*internally.* We also put together several company "Briefing

Books," using the financial and news services of the *Wall Street Journal*, which likewise challenged the bank's belief that its private banking customers had no real alternative source for investment advice. Within thirty minutes the committee had identified half a dozen new business opportunities, had begun rethinking the supposed efficiency of its back-office processes, and had authorized a number of projects with which to gather more information.

A critical feature of most successful technology introduction programs is the existence of a technology advocacy group, with the explicit mission of bringing unfamiliar applications inside and finding a context in which to demonstrate their potential. The British Post Office maintains a permanent technology research group championed by Director of Technology Duncan Hine and operated by Director of Research Alan Shepherd. This advocacy department, a model for any organization, is permanently staffed. Its mission is to facilitate the organization's understanding of new technologies and their implications.

More to the point, the Post Office Research Group takes an active, if not religious, role in promoting and accelerating technology adoption. In addition to coordinating the study tours we mentioned earlier, the group manages a technology innovation fund, produces six internal conferences a year (with attendance as high as 200 executives each, and complete with hands-on demos), publishes a regular newsletter, and coordinates the transfer of technology "lessons-learned" throughout the organization. Taking a counterlesson from their American counterparts, the British Post Office seems determined not to put itself out of business and recognizes the power of a finely tuned technology radar to help it survive.

Technology Partnerships

Building a killer app requires the formation of partnerships; as we said, the goal is to treat every transaction like a joint venture. Partnering is another natural side effect of the Law of Diminishing Firms. As firms find market partners who can perform functions cheaper and more effectively than they can themselves, the economically necessary response is to shift functions to these partners. In some cases the associated organization will be a familiar one—an existing supplier, a customer, or even a competitor or regulatory body—but the relationship will take on a dramatic new degree of intimacy. In other cases, the relationship will be with someone completely new.

For many organizations, the breadth and depth of these new partnerships can be intimidating. Large, integrated organizations (banks and utilities are good examples) may be unfamiliar with or even legally forbidden to have any connection that involves the exchange of proprietary information. Organizations in mature industries that have enjoyed long periods of stability (many durable goods producers, for example) may not have met a new player for a long time. They may have developed a kind of organizational xenophobia that makes them suspicious of any tie to an unfamiliar partner.

Even in industries and individual organizations where alliances and acquisitions are regular events, there are infamous stories of breakdowns that cost the respective organizations dearly, if only in bad publicity. During the 1980s, IBM was notorious for acquiring entrepreneurial companies and then crushing the life out of them with its self-referential corporate culture and daunting bureaucracy. More recently, the business press has had a field day describing the fireworks associated with on-again, off-again alliances, mergers, and divestitures of entertainment, communications, and technology giants like Time Warner (itself a painful alliance of two giants), AT&T, and Rupert Murdoch's News Corp.

It is particularly important to form technology partnerships, for these are at the heart of the innovation portfolio. Typically, this is an area that most organizations need to improve significantly before they can begin implementation or even development of their digital strategy. Even in organizations with excellent partnering skills, relations with technology suppliers are typically poor. At McDonald's, relations with upstream providers of raw materials are so crucial to satisfying the company's obsession with quality, consistency, and value that these companies are referred to not as business partners but as "McFamily." Yet McDonald's I/S personnel readily admitted their relationships with key providers like Microsoft, Lotus, and AT&T, each of which provides mission-critical components of its technology platform, were arm's length at best.

Understanding that its plans for more strategic applications would cause the company to rely even more on these and other vendors, McDonald's corporate I/S group staged a command performance in which these companies could meet with McDonald's management and with each other and begin to identify win-win opportunities that would take the relationships far beyond that of merely vendor and customer. As McDonald's executives began to think more strategically about technology, they also found themselves working with a kind of technology partner that was new to them—start-up companies. The nature of the company's relations with media partners, like its former lead national advertising agency, Leo Burnett, and a key licensing partner, Walt Disney, changed as well.

Sometimes it is the technology company that leads the partnership, a reflection of its own effort to unleash a killer app. In its move from a software company to a full-scale financial services firm in cyberspace, Intuit has developed an on-line marketplace for insurance, including quotations and applications, in cooperation with Allstate, State Farm, Prudential, and others. The company's site will soon offer a full-service mortgage brokerage as well, and some of the leading lenders in the country have already signed up. To secure its technology platform, the company purchased a 19 percent stake in the search engine Excite.

The CEO Agenda

Finding and introducing new technologies into an organization's collective consciousness feeds the process of digital strategy, and keeping a pipeline that is full and unfiltered maximizes the chances that something will come out at the other end with the potential to be a killer app. But for the technology pipeline to function, most organizations need to retool themselves in other significant ways.

Like an inactive person training for a new sport, organizations need to prepare for digital strategy before they can hope to succeed at it without too much trauma. Senior management must learn to accept that digital technology has become central to future planning and align its objectives with those parties in the organization who are today responsible for technology implementation, whether that is the I/S organization, an outsourcing partner, or managers in the field organization.

In the end, the real distinction between digital winners and losers is always found in the boardroom. At every client we've worked with on digital strategy, and for every organization we have visited or studied, it is always the case that those organizations which do not have the will to succeed are certain not to do so. That will must be internalized, communicated, and championed by the senior executive and the entire executive team. Inside each of the organizations who have used digital technology to achieve market dominance—whether at a FedEx, Playboy, or tomorrow's high-flying start-up—there are executives who believe in it and who have gone out of their way to communicate their convictions within and outside the organization.

At VEBA, our project began after CEO Ulrich Hartmann met Nicholas Negroponte and instinctively recognized that "being digital" was a requirement for his company to succeed in the twenty-first century, despite the fact that for more than a hundred years it had shown no signs of doing anything wrong. At British Petroleum, CEO John Browne knew better than to ask his directors to expand the company through technology leadership until he communicated his own commitment in no uncertain terms. Every employee at BP agrees to a "performance contract" with their boss, which contains the job criteria by which the employee agrees to be measured. In 1996, Browne made the company's success in digital technology innovation part of his own performance contract with his boss, the company's board of directors.

Digital strategy, like any strategy, requires fearless leadership. As Michael Bloomberg, CEO of the Bloomberg Financial Network, described his role in technology adoption: "If it doesn't work, you can blame me. There's no question about that."

9

the new operating model

In one sense, they are thinking backwards from the future, rather than tracing a path from here to there and becoming caught in the prediction trap.
—James Burke

WHENEVER WE ARE out preaching the gospel of digital strategy, one question comes up over and over again. "How do we make money on the Web?" (or with multimedia, global positioning systems, groupware, artificial intelligence, and so on). On the surface, it's a fair question. Venture capitalists, private investors, and thousands of companies seem hell-bent on pouring millions of dollars into developing and using new technologies without the slightest idea how they're going to come out. The *New York Times* greets hiccups in America Online's service or the closing of an ill-conceived Web site as signals that the momentum of digital technology may be slowing down. *Red Herring* and *Upside,* the leading investor-oriented technology magazines, have been searching obsessively for what they call the "Internet business model," as if the failure to find one, and find one soon, will mean the end of a very long and very joyous party in Silicon Valley. And even Robert Metcalfe predicted in 1996 that the Internet would collapse, in a column he was later forced to eat (literally).

But asking how to make money with new technology is asking the wrong question. It implies that the technology is some kind of printing press, which, if properly primed, will start producing revenue but which otherwise sits around doing nothing, an enormously expensive paperweight. The real question is, and always has been, "How do we make money?" As Donna Iucolano, who oversaw $30 million dollars in sales in 1996 over the Web for 1-800-Flowers, said recently, "People ask, 'What do you have to do to be a successful on-line merchant?' I think you really have to ask, 'What do you have to do to be a successful merchant?' It's really no different. You have to serve your customers, integrating everything that you do."

Just Do It

The people making money with digital technology are people who are just doing business, taking advantage of new technologies and their potential to cut costs (Moore's Law) or improve reach (Metcalfe's Law), and taking advantage of your hesitation. Their killer apps are not technology initiatives. They're business initiatives. These are companies whose managers don't actually understand the difference, because they believe their most underutilized and inexhaustible asset is information and their key weapon is digital technology. Some of these organizations don't even distinguish their I/S function from the operation of the business.

Silicon Valley companies like Hewlett-Packard, WebTV, and hundreds of software start-ups embody this new operating model. But you don't have to drive down Highway 101 to see it in action. Sports giant Nike has progressively divorced itself from everything that isn't a core process—production, distribution, advertising, and even design have been outsourced, managed through robust and high bandwidth communications channels. What Nike has kept for itself is brand management, the relentless development of the Nike world view, the Nike lifestyle and the Nike experience.

In 1994, CEO Phil Knight began expanding the company not just with more varieties of shoes but with apparel generally. "We decided we're a sports company, not just a shoe company," he said recently. And now the company is poised to take the next logical step, which is to reposition itself not as a sports company but as a services company, managing events for others. Nike's asset is its brand management expertise, not its production capacity, and Knight is moving to leverage that expertise. Nike is already living a digital strategy. In this chapter, we discuss a few of the key operating principles.

Explore Continuously

Exploring and exploiting your digital future are two faces of the same process, the process of prototyping. *Prototyping* is a concept borrowed from engineering, where functional and technical uncertainty encourages practitioners to build early versions of products and systems to ensure a basic fit between the requirements, materials, and environmental conditions in which the system must operate. Digital prototypes are required for the analogous reasons. In the uncertain business environment of the digital frontier, real-world evaluation of digital strategy prototypes is often the only means of testing and ensuring business value.

A prototype is sometimes thought of as merely a trial run of a new product or system; digital strategy prototypes are something very different. For one thing, the prototype is not necessarily a nonfunctioning version of a strategy. As technology becomes cheaper and standardized more quickly, it is now possible to build fully operational systems at minimal cost. Likewise, you may not want to throw the prototype away. The prototype may be the first of many iterations of a new good or service offering. Everything is a prototype, because nothing is ever finished.

Prototyping is the implementation paradigm for organizations that want to unleash killer apps. Prototypes test, refine, and ultimately commit the organization to pursue some subset of the ideas generated as part of digital strategy. This process involves many more members of the organization (ultimately all of them) and leads to the development of ideas in conjunction with partner organizations, including technology providers, traditional suppliers, and customers. The prototypes may be developed purely to test and demonstrate a single good or service, or they may be working models of an entirely new business that will formally spin out of the existing organization to develop the ideas independently.

During the first set of digital strategy exercises at McDonald's, electronic commerce emerged as a "painfully obvious" means of achieving many of the company's strategic objectives. The digital strategy team's wilder ideas included (1) improving customers' in-store experience by helping them find the nearest McDonald's while on the road and give food orders from the car, (2) using the Internet and public data sources to help McDonald's fine-tune purchasing, pricing, and menu decisions in real time, (3) and using the Web to open a new channel for marketing, recruiting, labor scheduling, and maybe even training (if, indeed, there was any difference between the four).

Fine ideas. But how to get started?

The team began simply. Representatives from the strategy teams began by meeting with Leo Burnett, McDonald's lead national advertising firm at the time, on the sensible assumption that this long-standing partner would be able to provide expertise on using new media effectively. Burnett, it turned out, had no experience with most of the new media, including the World Wide Web. Recognizing its lack of expertise, Burnett recommended partnering with America Online and a design company familiar with AOL's proprietary interface.

Working with AOL brought in a new partner, one with expertise in communicating digitally. Still, the team knew it did not have the experience to launch a full-fledged killer app and instead concentrated on a prototype that would expose McDonald's to both the medium and its users. The AOL site promoted the McDonald's brand as family friendly by offering an electronic information center and forum on parenting tips.

The AOL pilot was developed and launched, and response was good, if not overwhelming. One reason for the limited response may have been a mismatch of content and audience. McDonald's marketing is aimed as much at children as at parents and other adults, but the AOL site focused on the adults, because McDonald's believed they were more likely users of AOL than children. This was an assumption that additional market research might have helped to quantify, if not in fact contradict.

The AOL pilot had served its purpose as an experiment, however, and the team decided to take the next step. They went back to the drawing board and developed the first version of the company's corporate Web site. Six months later, the company launched the site, this time aiming more directly at children, offering games and an interactive coloring book. Children are invited to write E-mail directly to Ronald McDonald (a feature of the AOL pilot that had proven popular), who sends an immediate response that includes a joke. Soon after the launch, the site was enhanced to improve the animation, add content, and add recruiting information for franchisees.

Nothing this structured is required for a successful prototype. During the 1996 Christmas season there was a mad rush for the underproduced "Tickle-Me-Elmo" doll. It wasn't clear until after Thanksgiving that the product was going to be a monstrous hit, but within days entrepreneurs had taken advantage of the reach of the Internet to create clearing houses, auctions, and virtual support groups for grieving parents on the World Wide Web. By Christmas, naturally, all of the sites had become passé. These entrepreneurs were largely individuals with no business experience and certainly no strategic planning expertise. Within days they matched a market need to a technology solution, developed and launched their first experiments, and went through numerous revisions, from beginning to end. And yes, they made money.

Creating the Space

As these examples demonstrate, prototypes are not simply technical prototypes. They also challenge the organization to experiment
with new organizational models and confront stale corporate cul-
tures. McDonald's initially found itself in the unusual position of
having to convince its advertising firm that it ought to be taking
advantage of new and emerging media, and the ensuing joint
development not only changed the dynamic between the two
companies but also brought in new players who had previously
been unknown to both. With Tickle-Me-Elmo, many of the sellers
probably didn't even realize they could auction their products
until competitive bids started to come in.

Operating models and asset management assumptions are
also challenged by prototypes. A newspaper might decide its
future is in digital publishing, making obsolete its current physical and distribution resources. A wholesaler may decide its
future lies in getting out of wholesaling altogether and instead
using digital technology to offer outsourced logistics support
for its customers. These new incarnations will not come without
a lot of pain.

The organization may be stoical enough to develop the new
organization from within the structure and systems of the existing organization. (That is certainly what Bill Gates has been
doing for the past two years at Microsoft, but software, after all,
is a lot more plastic than a factory.) If not, the executive team
must be prepared to recommend that development occur in a
protected space, whether it be a skunk works team operating at
a remote location or perhaps a new subsidiary, financed in cooperation with new partners.

Gordon Bell calls such protected spaces "intraventures" and
the people who work them "intrapreneurs." He and his business
partner, Heidi Mason, work closely with companies to help
them set up and operate such ventures successfully. At the core
of this work is the Bell-Mason Diagnostic, a sophisticated expert
system that evaluates the risks associated with the new venture
on twelve critical dimensions. At key stages in the venture's life

cycle, the diagnostic is used to compare the state of the venture with that of hundreds of others in a database, allowing Bell and Mason to quickly determine when and where problem areas are likely to emerge.

The risk of failing adequately to protect the space within which the prototypes are developing is to continually try to force the future into the paradigms of the present. It's fine for virtual shopping malls like BarclaySquare to begin with a simplified digital reproduction of the current understanding of what retail shopping is (stores, items, shopping baskets, checkout), but that model must quickly evolve to reflect the new environment of cyberspace or risk looking quaint. MCI Marketplace, another cybermall, never developed beyond simply offering online catalogs of its merchant customers, and the site grew stale, ultimately leading MCI to close it. Barclays, on the other hand, continues to look for new ways to use the technology available to offer new features of the shopping experience.

Or consider comic book publisher Marvel Entertainment Group, which has undertaken cannibalistic experiments in digital production and distribution. The company made a remarkable discovery a few years ago when it *pre*released the first issue of a new comic book title on the World Wide Web weeks before it saw print. Since comic books are now colored digitally, the content was already available; in fact, the coloring is so advanced that the pages looked even better on the screen. The buzz generated by this experiment actually sold more copies of the "real" comic book, sales of which broke records.

The company has since institutionalized its digital experiments, releasing an on-line only "cybercomic" weekly over America Online, soon to be released over the Web. From a humble experiment, Marvel learned a valuable lesson. It is a lesson about information assets. The real value of a "content" company lies not in the number of artifacts (software packages, magazines, videotapes, and so on) it can sell, but in how it can get the most leverage from its intellectual property—in the case of Marvel, its characters and stories. As the experiment suggests, that leverage may in the end completely change the company's value chain.

Turning on a Bit

As you develop prototypes, you refine your vision and begin the process of realizing it. At this point organizations find it is no longer possible even to separate the digital strategy from the previous strategy or from the current operations or business model of the organization. Talking about a relationship changes the relationship. Imagining your future creates a new future.

The final "step" in unleashing killer apps is really not a step at all but simply a continuation of what you've been doing. The prototypes become more focused and more sophisticated, and they continue to integrate new technologies that help achieve the goals you set. They become increasingly "public," in that more of your business partners begin to use them, either as a supplemental channel or a replacement channel for current transactions.

To succeed with a digital strategy, renewal must be a constant. If you've launched a home page on the Web, it is imperative to revisit and adjust it continually, not only to maintain customer interest but also to get rid of things that aren't working and replace them with new prototypes that might. This is a developing principle of all information systems, not just mission-critical ones but supporting ones as well. Big releases are risky, and as Moore's Law changes the technology landscape with increased speed, they become unfeasible. The technology mutates too fast to be in development with a fixed structure for very long. At Wal-Mart, new "releases" of core store systems like accounting and inventory are deployed *every 90 days*. If you don't think your organization can handle that much disruption, think again. It is the only way.

Fortunately, digital technology is extremely malleable, and the emerging open platforms are dramatically improving interoperability of software components and reducing the reliance on individual vendors. Any computer can be an Internet host and/or an Internet client. All the tools that are part of the World Wide Web, including audio, animation, real-time video, three-dimensional modeling, and the distributed Java programming environment, run on nearly every platform. New releases cause less trauma because the technology is improving to make it so.

Examples of such "extended delivery" solutions are everywhere, and you need only spend one or two hours a week surfing the Web to see them. The best sites are constantly being refreshed and enhanced. Amazon seems to add new features every week, and the FedEx site has been overhauled at least twice in the last twelve months. Many sites use news, contests, and customer feedback to generate new material and new users. Match.com, an electronic dating service, began by giving users the opportunity to post personal profiles and match themselves with other users based on a variety of criteria. Match.com then acted as a go-between by rerouting E-mail directed at its anonymous users to the actual participants. The system has been upgraded over time to add chat rooms, more intelligent searching, an agent-based E-mail service to inform users when new profiles they might find interesting are posted, and, recently, the ability to place anonymous phone calls to other members.

Sometimes it is the entire organization that shifts direction, not just its outside interface. We have followed closely a small software company called VREAM, started in the one-bedroom apartment of former McKinsey consultant Ed LaHood in 1991. LaHood believed that virtual reality interfaces could be developed for and on the cheapest desktop computers rather than the high-end workstations his competitors relied on, and he set about to build a product that would allow users to create manipulable, three-dimensional worlds. His original product sold for $1,000 and ran on PCs running Microsoft Windows, and it did everything done by products that cost ten times as much and ran only on high-end graphics workstations.

VREAM did moderately well selling its product through various non-retail channels. And then the World Wide Web came along. With the success of Netscape, LaHood recognized the power of this new environment to distribute good software quickly and cheaply. It was an opportunity that he couldn't pass up. Overnight, the development team shifted gears and began rewriting the product to work on the Web and follow the Web's open virtual reality software standard.

Within months, VREAM had a working model, and was one of the first virtual reality products to be included as a plug-in extension to Netscape's Web browser. In its first month of release, the new product was downloaded 30,000 times. The viewer and a series of amazing demonstrations were given away, and the company now makes its revenue by selling the authoring tool and assisting clients to build their own applications. The company was acquired in 1996 by Platinum Technology, in part to help Platinum migrate its own suite of client-server application products to the Web using VREAM's interface. ·

Mike Backes, founder of game developer Rocket Science, tells a similar story. Founded with much fanfare by this visionary Hollywood producer and writer, Rocket Science's original mission was to capitalize on Moore's Law by creating digitally produced video games with the look and feel of a major motion picture.

The initial product, as Backes readily admits, was a flop. "It turns out that you can't give away point of view and still tell a story," Backes told us. Rocket Science was building games for children, and children are not patient. They will not read a manual. The company had been determined to tell stories through its games, but that proved impossible.

Rather than giving up, the staff tried another strategy. This time, they decided to follow the rules of the video game market but bring to it the production values of Hollywood movies—the attention to detail, the focus on overall experience, and the glamour. The business model was to build high-end games for devices that didn't yet exist, but that were coming from Sony, Sega, and Nintendo. Rocket Science began developing a game that would run on a machine that could handle 500,000 frames of animation and be played by multiple users over a network that didn't even exist. But by the time this first new product, Obsidian, was ready to ship, so was the machine.

In unleashing killer apps, dramatic changes in the middle of implementation are not unusual, nor are they the career-ending events they were in the days of closed systems and slower-moving developments in technology. VREAM changed the hardware and software platform of its product as well as its revenue model and its customer base; even its advertising, distribution, sales, marketing, and support were radically altered.

All in a day's work.

Unleashing the Power of Communications

Change, as organizational psychologists like to say, is stress. Organizations, like individuals, find the best way for managing stress is to communicate about it. The broader the channel and the wider the audience, the easier it is to move not just senior executives but every participant in an organization's prototypes— employees, suppliers, and customers alike—into the future right along with the business model.

Every large company has a phone system, internal mail, and other forms of regular and ad hoc communications. But organizations that want to succeed in digital strategy understand that these channels must be interoperable, robust, and based on open architectures and standardized tools, not only for cost advantage and easy replacement, but also for the ability to extend communications with outside stakeholders. Does your organization have an "E-mail culture"? Is it adequately supported? How hard would it be to add voice, video, document sharing, and other collaborative tools? The Internet supports all of this today for a completely ad hoc group of global participants, and they never have to make out a budget.

The best way to build the channel is to use the technologies that are causing the disruption. As the first and most obvious implementation of their digital strategy, many organizations we have worked with chose to restructure their internal and external communications architectures around open standards and the global computing environment of the Internet. This becomes the new platform from which their killer apps are launched.

Building and deploying company networks using these standards not only saves money but also expands exponentially the potential linkages with buyers, suppliers, investors, and other business partners. The business case for doing so, especially compared with clumsy, expensive, and unsatisfying current networks, is often a no-brainer. The NASDAQ market advertises that it now operates entirely using Internet standards on a dedicated network (a so-called intranet). As marketers at Sun Microsystems put it, "The Internet is where you make money. Intranets are where you save money."

If you think this is a strategy that's plausible only for high-tech companies in California, think again. At its technology symposium in January 1996, several of British Petroleum's senior executives were struck by a presentation from Hewlett-Packard on standardizing desktops around a common operating environment (COE), which included the systems software, communications architecture, and basic applications such as E-mail and groupware. BP's CEO John Browne was ready to announce a major reorganization that would decentralize it even further and prepare it for new growth, and he knew that the communications infrastructure, disparate within and across divisions, with multiple and incompatible hardware and software, was not suitably robust to play the critical role he had in mind for it. (A few days after the colloquium, Browne demonstrated the organization's growing need for an integrated communications network. He sent an E-mail message to the entire company, to which he attached a memo describing the new structure. As he expected, 20 percent of the intended recipients never got the E-mail, and more than half couldn't access the attachment.)

Excitement about the idea of a COE for BP spread rapidly, and within a few days the senior executives met with Browne and Group I/T Director John Cross, who had organized the symposium. The group estimated that full implementation would cost over $150 million, a capital expense the group had no doubt would return instantly to the bottom line. How fast could it be done? Cross said the total rollout, which meant changing over 35,000 desktop systems, could take up to three years. But the executive team opted instead for a higher-speed implementation.

Cross formed a small development team, which settled on the architecture for the new environment within a couple of months. BP Exploration, one of three divisions, committed implementation funds immediately, and rolled out its first wave of COE desktops by the fall. A little over a year after BP senior executives had heard the presentation from HP, all of BP Exploration had been converted.

As of mid-1997, the worldwide rollout for all divisions was halfway done, and scheduled for completion by the end of the year. The COE must be responsive to the Law of Disruption, however, and the plan is to roll out upgrades every six to nine months, all done electronically and "hands-free" from a central distribution point. Next year's goal is to get the time from upgrade distribution to complete implementation on all 35,000 desktops down to one month.

The COE effort has been one of BP's most successful I/S projects ever. Users aren't just pleased with the system, they're fervent in their praise. The E-mail systems are not only unified but work with "lightning speed." According to project leader Phiroz Darukhanavala, "Messages now go around the world in seconds, not minutes. Sometimes it feels like an on-line dialogue is going on in real time." And, he says, the standardization has given BP a new sense of unity. "At any BP office in the world, I know I'm only two clicks away from my own desk. One click to turn on the machine, one to connect an ethernet cable. And if there's no BP office, I just dial into one. It's usually a local call." Managers now regularly take their laptop computers when traveling and use them to extend the reach of meetings beyond those who are physically in attendance. "I knew COE had made it," Darukhanavala told us, "when they started sending me messages like, 'The spirit of COE is being felt in this room.'"

The insight of a handful of senior executives at a technology futures symposium changed not only the operating model of a global, industrial-age organization, but opened new channels for interaction between staff members who are spread to the four corners of the earth. This has greatly facilitated the move to a flatter organization. The project has also changed the attitude of many senior executives about what an I/S organization can really do, and do quickly, for the company.

BP's COE is surely a killer app, and the speed and ease with which the organization found, developed, and implemented it surprises even those who did the work. It's ironic that we begin and end with BP, a decidedly industrial-age company making tremendous headway in the digital age: first as an example of digital strategy happening in the field, without the participation of company headquarters, and then, a year later, as a story of senior management leadership.

When organizations—regardless of size, locality, or age—decide to live in the new world, and when they have leaders who are willing to travel to the edge of the digital frontier themselves and assure everyone else that it's safe to cross, Moore's Law, Metcalfe's Law, and the power of Coasean economics are transformed, turned from disruptive forces into beneficent ones, helping organizations create order out of chaos and new value out of old information. "Visitors keep asking us for the templates we used to calculate return on investment," concludes Darukhanavala. "We don't have any. We're spending 150 million dollars based on a vision."

10

lighting out for
the territories

We'll survive because we're basically completely insane.
—Laurie Anderson

THE **CONVERGENCE** of new digital technologies in the past five years has created an environment rich enough to support life in all forms—social, familial, and political as well as business. As we have suggested throughout this book, this new world of cyberspace will increasingly be the place where business is transacted, customers are contacted, and wealth created and distributed.

As we write these pages, cyberspace still exhibits characteristics long associated with rapidly-settling frontiers, including its lack of and resistance to complex regulation and law, its open and democratic nature, and its primitive living conditions. Some, like John Perry Barlow, hope and expect that cyberspace will always retain these frontier features, as advances in digital technology fueled by Moore's Law and

Metcalfe's Law continue to push virtual life further and further from its physical counterpart. If this is the case, then understanding the nature of frontier society is a critical skill for anyone hoping to do business there. This is particularly important for anyone over the age of 30, whom Barlow refers to as the "immigrants" of cyberspace. It is the next generation, those who will spend their adult lives never having known the absence of the Internet, who are the "natives" of cyberspace. The natives are already restless, and are beginning to flex their economic muscle. Before long they'll make up not only your customers but your employees, shareholders, and, yes, even your managers and senior executives.

A little over a hundred years ago, at the Chicago World's Columbian Exposition, historian Frederick Jackson Turner delivered a paper that changed the course of historical studies of the New World. The North American frontier had officially closed, Turner said, and it was time to recognize the role its settlement had played not only in American society but in Western Europe as well. In "The Significance of the Frontier in American History," Turner argued that the frontier—the "meeting point between savagery and civilization"—*was* the American experience, and that as it advanced it "carried with it individualism, democracy, and nationalism, and powerfully affected the East and the Old World." The frontier spurred the development of the modern world: politically, economically, and socially. "The wilderness," he wrote, "masters the colonist."

Turner may as well have been speaking about cyberspace. Whereas the American West was fueled by free land, cyberspace is fueled by free computing power and free bandwidth (thanks to Moore) and free software (thanks to Metcalfe). In both cases, the social conditions that resulted are raw, and the nature of the business climate, by necessity, less developed. As Turner wrote, "A primitive society can hardly be expected to show the intelligent appreciation of the complexity of business interests in a developed society."

Many popular conceptions of the American West are greatly romanticized versions of what really happened, but in essence we believe the analogy of cyberspace as a new frontier is apt. The

West was not lawless, and neither is cyberspace, though both are perceived that way by outsiders—especially those from the old world who would govern them. What is true is that the West adapted, sometimes crudely, legal and commercial traditions of the East and of the Old World and often delivered its justice, regulated its commerce, and settled its property disputes in a swift and efficient fashion suited to the climate of rapid change.

Similarly, even as local, national, and international governments try, and fail, to assert their own legal regimes on the frontier of cyberspace, a native regulatory framework, adapted from the laws of the rest of the world and appropriate to the very different physics, economics, and business environment of this new frontier, is emerging. As with new markets of the past, cyberspace is developing a commercial code of conduct that is largely self-regulating and based more on common-sense custom and practice than on an impossible jumble of laws and regulations from every jurisdiction in the world. The Cyberspace Law Institute, a virtual body of professors and practitioners, has launched a Virtual Magistrate project to provide a low-cost dispute resolution mechanism that takes advantage of technology to resolve problems related to its use. And the Electronic Frontier Foundation, founded by John Perry Barlow and Lotus founder Mitch Kapor, is cyberspace's advocate and unofficial ambassador to the governments of the physical world, equal parts John Muir and Davy Crockett.

Given the unsettled nature of cyberspace and the likelihood that in some fashion it will always remain so, what is an entrepreneur, or an entrepreneurial manager, to do? One response, the response we have described in this book, is simply to move there and start doing business. Those who make the transformation by developing a digital strategy are choosing to engage the frontier on its own terms, just as their counterparts from Europe did in settling the New World. These include explorers, traders, homesteaders, and ranchers, as well as railroad magnates, land speculators, and mineral barons—the John Jacob Astors, Cornelius Vanderbilts, and John Rockefellers.

We have met examples of each of these characters already. They include the founders of America Online, Barclays Bank, and the enthusiastic young employees of Rocket Science and virtual bookseller Amazon.com. (FedEx is the Wells Fargo of cyberspace, and Wells Fargo is itself the land office where the gold is kept.) The telephone, satellite, cellular, and cable companies are surely playing out the same high drama of boom-and-bust infrastructure development as did the American railroads in the 1800s. The players change, but the roles remain largely the same. "Those who cannot remember the past are condemned to repeat it," wrote George Santayana. On the other hand, those who study the past can avoid a hell of a lot of mistakes.

The development of electronic commerce and digital society are likewise following with remarkable similarity the development of resource-rich frontiers in the physical world, operating in the sped-up time of Internet years. There are rogues, heroes, philanthropists, entrepreneurs. There are big winners and big losers, fortunes made and lost, and killer apps providing the equivalent randomness of a giant gold strike or a railroad's routing around a booming city and reducing it, overnight, to a ghost town.

From our own dispatches and those of our colleagues, we have tried in this book to paint a picture of how the new business environment is evolving, of the economics that motivate it, and of the nascent set of rules, principles, and operating models that have indicated—so far—who wins and who loses in the struggle to unleash the next killer app.

If, after reading these frontier stories, you decide you'd rather not go west, remember that cyberspace, like the North American frontier, was more a state of mind than a physical location. Both are filled with so much creative energy that they naturally dominate their respective old worlds. With cyberspace, thanks to the Law of Disruption and the new forces, the transformation of today's markets, customers, and channels is happening with breathtaking speed. There's really no way to avoid the future, except maybe, as some frustrated CEOs we know have suggested, to retire. (And even there you'll find no refuge, but that's another story.)

A bus driver from Houston recently test "drove" a prototype stretch of Interstate 15 in San Diego that has been transformed via digital technology into an autopia, where the road, not the drivers, controls the cars. "I love it," he said. "At first it was a little scary, but after five minutes, you get used to it."

Five minutes is precisely how long you have to react to these developments. So you have got to do something. By outlining the process of digital strategy, explaining the twelve design principles, and describing the experiences of organizations that are transforming themselves so they can unleash killer apps, we have suggested what we believe to be the best response available. It is the response, you can rest assured, of your competitors—if not the traditional ones, then certainly those that are rapidly approaching your blind spot.

If you follow only one recommendation from this book, follow the one suggested to sociologist Sherry Turkle by the thirteen-year-old she observed playing SimLife. "Just play."

world wide web addresses

This appendix provides current addresses (URLs) for many of the organizations mentioned in this book.

AltaVista	www.altavista.digital.com
Amazon.com Books	www.amazon.com
American Express	www.americanexpress.com
America Online	www.aol.com
Apple Computers	www.apple.com
AT&T	www.att.com
Auto-by-Tel	www.autobytel.com
Backroads	www.backroads.com
Barclays Group	www.barclays.co.uk
Barnes & Noble	www.barnesandnoble.com
Barter Systems	www.bartersys.com
Bellcore	www.bellcore.com
Bowne & Co.	www.bowne.com
British Petroleum PLC	www.bp.com
The British Post Office	www.uk-po.com
Charles Schwab	www.schwab.com
ChemSource/ChemConnect	www.chemconnect.com
Cisco Systems	www.cisco.com
C|Net	www.cnet.com
Compaq	www.compaq.com
CompuServe	world.compuserve.com

Cornell Law School	www.law.cornell.edu
Cornell Supreme Court Database	supct.law.cornell.edu/supct
CyberCash	www.cybercash.com
Cyberspace Law Institute	www.cli.org
Daimler-Benz	www.mercedes.com
Dallas Morning News	www.dallasnews.com
Dell Computers	www.dell.com
Diamond Technology Partners	www.diamtech.com
DigiCash	www.digicash.com
Digital City	www.digitalcity.com
Digital Knowledge Assets	www.dkaweb.com
Disney	www.disney.com
Dutch PTT	www.ptt-telecom.nl
E*Trade	www.etrade.com
EDGAR Database	www.sec.gov/edaux/searches.htm
Electronic Frontier Foundation	www.eff.org
Encarta Online	encarta.msn.com
Encyclopedia Britannica Online	www.eb.com
Ernie	ernie.ey.com
ESPN SportsZone	espn.sportszone.com
Excite	www.excite.com
FedEx	www.fedex.com
FedWorld Information Network	www.fedworld.gov
Firefly	www.firefly.com
Four11 Directory Services	www.four11.com
General Magic	www.genmagic.com
GetSmart	www.getsmart.com
Glasgow Electric	www.glasgow-ky.com/epb
Hallmark Electronic Greetings	www.hallmarkconnections.com
Hambrecht & Quist	www.hambrecht.com
Hewlett-Packard	www.hp.com
Holiday Inn	www.res.holiday-inn.com
Hüls AG	www.huels.de
IBM	www.ibm.com

ICQ	www.icq.com
Intel	www.intel.com
InterNIC	www.internic.net
Intuit	www.intuit.com
IRS	www.irs.ustreas.gov
Kleiner Perkins Caufield & Byers	www.kpcb.com
Lens 4 Me	www.lens4me.com
Leo Burnett	www.leoburnett.com
LEXIS-NEXIS	www.lexis.com
Library of Congress	lcweb.loc.gov
LiveLink	www.livelink.com
Lotus Development Corporation	www.lotus.com
Marshall Industries	www.marshall.com
Marvel Entertainment Group	www.marvel.com
Mastercard	www.mastercard.com
Match.Com	www.match.com
McDonald's	www.mcdonalds.com
McKinsey & Company	www.mckinsey.com
Microsoft	www.microsoft.com
MIT Media Laboratory	www.media.mit.edu
Mobil Corporation	www.mobil.com
Mondex	www.mondex.com
The Motley Fool	www.fool.com
Motorola	www.mot.com
National Basketball Association	www.nba.com
Netscape	home.netscape.com
The New York Times	www.nyt.com
Nike	www.nike.com
Nintendo	www.nintendo.com
1-800-Flowers	www.1800flowers.com
Oracle	www.oracle.com
o.tel.o	www.o-tel-o.de
The Palace	www.thepalace.com
Peapod	www.peapod.com

Platinum Technology (VREAM)	www.platinum.com
Playboy	www.playboy.com
PlumbNet	www.plumbnet.com
PointCast	www.pointcast.com
Quicken Financial Network	www.quicken.com
QuickQuote	www.quickquote.com
The Red Herring	www.herring.com
Rocket Science Games	www.rocketsci.com
Saatchi & Saatchi	www.saatchibuscomm.com
San Jose Mercury News	www.sjmercury.com
Security First Network Bank	www.sfnb.com
Sega	www.sega.com
Simon & Schuster	www.superlibrary.com
Sony	www.sony.com
Stanford University	www.stanford.edu
Starwave	www.starwave.com
Sun Microsystems	www.sun.com
Sydkraft	www.sydkraft.se
THOMAS	thomas.loc.gov
Time Warner	www.timewarner.com
Toyota	www.toyota.com
Travelocity	www.travelocity.com
United Airlines	www.ual.com
United States Postal Service	www.usps.com
UPS	www.ups.com
Upside Magazine	www.upside.com
U.S. Patent and Trademark Office	www.uspto.gov
UtiliCorp United	www.utilicorp.com
VEBA AG	www.veba.de
Viacom	www.viacom.com
Visual Properties	www.visualproperties.com
Wall Street Journal	www.wsj.com
Wal-Mart	www.wal-mart.com

WebTV	www.webtv.net
Wells Fargo	www.wellsfargo.com
West Group	www.westgroup.com
Wildfire Communications	www.wildfire.com
Wit Capital	www.witcapital.com
XS4ALL	www.xs4all.nl
Yahoo!	www.yahoo.com

selected
bibliography

Adams, Scott. *The Dilbert Principle*. New York: HarperBusiness, 1996.

Brooks, Frederick P., Jr. *The Mythical Man-Month*. Reading: Addison-Wesley, 1975.

Brown, John Seely, ed. *Seeing Differently*. Boston: Harvard Business School Press, 1997.

Burke, James. *Connections*. Boston: Little Brown & Co, 1978.

Cameron, Julia. *The Vein of Gold*. New York: Putnam, 1996.

Coase, Ronald H. *Essays on Economics and Economists*. Chicago: University of Chicago Press, 1994.

———. *The Firm, the Market, and the Law*. Chicago: University of Chicago Press, 1988.

———. "My Evolution as an Economist." Unpublished lecture in the "Lives of the Laureates" series, given at Trinity University, San Antonio, Texas, April 12, 1994.

———. "The Nature of the Firm: Origin," *Journal of Law, Economics, and Organization* 4, no. 3 (1988).

Denning, Peter J., and Robert M. Metcalfe, eds. *Beyond Calculation*. New York: Springer-Verlag, 1997.

Drucker, Peter F. *Concept of the Corporation*. Rev. ed. New Brunswick: Transaction Publishers, 1993.

———. *Post-Capitalist Society*. New York: HarperBusiness, 1993.

Friedlander, Amy. *Emerging Infrastructure: The Growth of Railroads*. Reston, Va.: Corporation for National Research Initiatives, 1995.

————. *Natural Monopoly and Universal Service*. Reston, Va.: Corporation for National Research Initiatives, 1995.

Gallwey, Timothy. *The Inner Game of Tennis*. Rev. ed. New York: Random House, 1994.

Hagel, John III, and Arthur G. Armstrong. *Net Gain*. Boston: Harvard Business School Press, 1997.

Hamel, Gary. "Killer Strategies that Make Shareholders Rich." *Fortune*, 23 June 1997.

Hamel, Gary, and C. K. Prahalad. *Competing for the Future*. Boston: Harvard Business School Press, 1994.

Hammer, Michael, and James Champy. *Reengineering the Corporation*. New York: HarperBusiness, 1993.

Kelly, Kevin. *Out of Control*. Reading: Addison-Wesley, 1994.

Kuhn, Thomas S. *The Structure of Scientific Revolutions*. 3d. ed. Chicago: University of Chicago Press, 1996.

Leiber, Ronald B. "Just Redo It." *Fortune*, 23 June 1997.

McLuhan, Marshall, and Quentin Fiore. *The Medium Is the Massage*. New York: Bantam Books, 1967.

Mintzberg, Henry. *The Rise and Fall of Strategic Planning*. New York: Free Press, 1994.

Negroponte, Nicholas. *Being Digital*. New York: Alfred A. Knopf, 1995.

Pine, Joseph II. *Mass Customization*. Boston: Harvard Business School Press, 1993.

Porter, Michael E. *Competitive Advantage*. New York: Free Press, 1980.

————. "What Is Strategy?" *Harvard Business Review*, November–December 1996.

Posner, Richard A. *Sex and Reason*. Boston: Harvard University Press, 1992.

Quinn, James Brian. *The Intelligent Enterprise*. New York: Free Press, 1992.

Rayport, Jeffrey F., and John J. Sviokla. "Exploiting the Virtual Value Chain." *Harvard Business Review*, November–December 1995.

————. "Managing in the Marketspace." *Harvard Business Review*, November–December 1994.

Stigler, George J. *The Organization of Industry*. Chicago: University of Chicago Press, 1968.

Taylor, Frederick Winslow. *The Principles of Scientific Management*. New York: W. W. Norton & Co., 1967.

Treacy, Michael, and Fred Wiersema. *The Discipline of Market Leaders*. Reading, Mass.: Addison-Wesley, 1995.

Turner, Frederick Jackson. *The Frontier in American History*. New York: Dover, 1996.

White, Lynn Jr. *Medieval Technology and Social Change*. London: Oxford University Press, 1962.

index

about the authors

LARRY DOWNES is an independent consultant, lawyer, and teacher. In nearly twenty years of professional practice, he has worked with leading consulting firms, including Andersen Consulting, McKinsey & Co., and CSC Index, where he managed large-scale information systems development, emerging technology research, and strategy development on behalf of leading global businesses. He teaches courses on law and technology at Northwestern University and is a visiting fellow of the Diamond Exchange, an executive forum that brings together senior executives with leading strategy, technology, and learning experts. He can be reached at ldownes@killer-apps.com.

CHUNKA MUI is a partner with Diamond Technology Partners, director of the Diamond Exchange, and executive editor of the business magazine *Context*. The common thread that links all of Chunka's responsibilities is the goal of helping organizations evolve their business strategy in the context of both the new capabilities resulting from and the marketplace disruptions caused by digital technologies. He can be reached at chunka@diamtech.com.